Anglo-Zulu War 1879

COMBAT

British Infantryman
VERSUS
Zulu Warrior

Ian Knight

First published in Great Britain in 2013 by Osprey Publishing,
Osprey Publishing, PO Box 883, Oxford, OX1 9PL, UK
Osprey Publishing, PO Box 3985, New York, NY
10185-3985, USA

E-mail: info@ospreypublishing.com

OSPREY PUBLISHING IS PART OF THE OSPREY GROUP

A CIP catalogue record for this book is available from the British
Library

Print ISBN: 978 1 78200 365 6
PDF ebook ISBN: 978 1 47280 609 3
ePub ebook ISBN: 978 1 47280 610 9

Index by Alan Thatcher
Typeset in Univers, Sabon and Adobe Garamond Pro
Maps by bounford.com
Artwork by Peter Dennis
Originated by PDQ Media, Bungay, UK
Printed in China through Asia Pacific Offset Ltd.

13 14 15 16 17   10 9 8 7 6 5 4 3 2 1

Osprey Publishing is supporting the Woodland Trust, the UK's
leading woodland conservation charity, by funding the dedication
of trees.

www.ospreypublishing.com

Dedication

To Carolyn, Alex and Libby.

Editor's note

For ease of comparison please refer to the following conversion
table:

1 mile = 1.6km
1yd = 0.9m
1ft = 0.3m
1in = 2.54cm/25.4mm
1lb = 0.45kg

Artist's note

Readers may care to note that the original paintings from which
the artwork in this book was prepared are available for private
sale. All reproduction copyright whatsoever is retained by the
Publishers. All inquiries should be addressed to:

Peter Dennis, 'Fieldhead', The Park, Mansfield, Nottinghamshire
NG18 2AT, UK, or email magie.h@ntlworld.com

The Publishers regret that they can enter into no correspondence
upon this matter.

Key to military symbols

Key to unit identification

CONTENTS

Introduction

On 31 December 1878, Cpl Andrew Guthrie of the 90th Light Infantry, then on active service in southern Africa, reflected in his diary on what lay ahead. 'This is the last day of 1878', he wrote, 'and a long year before us. And a Zulu war to finish before we can think of a change for the better, [for other] than hard ground for a bed, sleeping in our clothes every night' (quoted in Macdougall 1998: 53). Guthrie had been in the British Army for two years, and had spent almost a year of it in Africa, where he had seen action in the dreary closing stages of the 9th Cape Frontier War, the last instalment of a century-old conflict between the expanding European settlement at the Cape of Good Hope and a robust African society, the Xhosa, whose territory lay across their line of advance. Now, with a new war brewing, he expressed no curiosity, either, about the new enemy; no doubt, like most of his comrades, he thought that he already had the measure of everything southern Africa could throw against him.

Guthrie's expectations of the coming year were widely shared and it was common knowledge among the troops that a Zulu campaign was imminent. In Zululand, too, the rising political tension was equally evident. The Zulu king, Cetshwayo kaMpande, recognized that underneath the increasingly belligerent British posturing lay broader policies, and several times across the second half of 1878 he assembled his *amabutho* – the part-time citizen militias which constituted the Zulu army – in a show of strength and defiance. This was deeply unsettling to the population at large. While the king and his council shied away from a direct confrontation, many young men by the end of 1878 were feeling deeply frustrated, and John Dunn – a white trader and hunter who enjoyed a privileged access to the Zulu court – noted that they increasingly directed their anger at the handful of whites who remained within the country. The king, he said 'had two regiments up before him in order to

talk war, and lay wagers, and challenge each other, as was their custom when preparing for war', and from

> … my camp I could see the gathering, which broke up in an unusual manner, as the soldiers shouted in an excited way, and a great number left their usual course and came in the direction of my camp … The soldiers of the gathering came swarming past, and several went right through my tents. On my speaking to them, they shouted out, 'That is past (meaning my authority); a white man is nothing now in this country; we will stab him with an assegai and disembowel him.' (Quoted in Moodie 1888: II. 493)

The road to Zululand – an unidentified British infantry battalion photographed in Pietermaritzburg, the colonial capital of Natal, *c.* 1879, drawn up in companies with the band to one side. Their generally smart appearance will not long survive the rigours of active service. (Author's Collection)

By the beginning of January 1879, the stage was increasingly set for the bloodiest confrontation yet between an indigenous society in southern Africa and the European interlopers. Since 1806, when a British force had captured a pro-French Dutch colony at the Cape in order to secure strategic maritime routes to India, Britain had found itself drawn deeper into Africa. By the 1870s, seeking to isolate the two large and antagonistic republics founded by Boer (Dutch) settlers in the interior, the British extended their control along the eastern seaboard. Both British and Boers had clashed frequently with the

9 Pounder shelling the enemy

V. Lloyd.

A Skirmish on Picquet.

A skirmish on the Eastern Cape Frontier. Fighting in this theatre in 1877–78 provided the British with a tactical blueprint for the early stages of their invasion of Zululand. A Royal Artillery gun supports an infantry skirmish-line – note the men lying firing beyond – while a detachment of Mounted Infantry mounts an attack to secure the flank. Similar tactics were employed at both Nyezane and iSandlwana, but were later abandoned in favour of more concentrated formations. (Author's Collection)

indigenous African societies who had occupied the land before them, while the discovery of diamonds north of the Cape in the 1860s added a financial element to what was already a cockpit of well-established rivalries.

London decided to bring the various disparate groups under overall British control, and in 1877 annexed the Transvaal Republic (but not the Orange Free State); a new High Commissioner, Sir Henry Bartle Frere, was dispatched to the Cape to implement the new policy, called Confederation. Frere had scarcely arrived when the last desperate rising of the Xhosa took place, sparking the 9th Cape Frontier War, and soon became convinced that Confederation could not succeed until the region's African population was compliant. For this reason he deliberately targeted the Zulu kingdom, the most powerful African independent society remaining in southern Africa, which lay north of the British colony of Natal. Although previous relations between the British and Zulu had largely been friendly, Frere seized on minor border infringements to present an ultimatum to Cetshwayo in December 1878.

The senior British commander in southern Africa at the end of 1878 was Lt-Gen Lord Chelmsford, an active man in his early 50s with a good deal of practical military experience behind him. Having inherited the closing stages of the 9th Cape Frontier War from his predecessor, Chelmsford had successfully winkled out the last defiant Xhosa bands from their natural mountain strongholds; this had deeply influenced his approach to southern African warfare. Although Chelmsford had commissioned an intelligence

Flank attack by the Mounted Infantry.

report into the nature of the Zulu army early in 1878 – long before London officially considered war a possibility – which had concluded that its organization and strengths were very different from those of the Xhosa, he remained convinced that they would react similarly under fire.

From the first, Chelmsford conceived his strategy for the invasion of Zululand as one of containment; never doubting that he could defeat the Zulu if he caught them, he felt his imperative was rather to bring a fast-moving and potentially elusive enemy to open battle. To this end, he planned on invading Zululand from several points along its borders, his columns converging on King Cetshwayo's principal residence, oNdini (which the British also knew as Ulundi).

Cetshwayo had been well aware throughout 1878 of the increasingly belligerent attitude of his British neighbours, and he assembled his army in January 1879. Not until British troops had actually crossed into Zulu territory, however, did he order them to undergo the necessary rituals to prepare them for battle, thereby committing himself to a military response to the invasion, and he weighed up his strategic options in council with his most trusted advisers and generals. The Zulu army needed clear objectives to attack and destroy, but Cetshwayo himself was reluctant to fight beyond his borders for fear of widening the conflict and diluting his moral position as the victim of British aggression. The strategy arrived at by the king and his counsellors was, therefore, both strategically defensive and tactically aggressive – the Zulu army would attack the British as quickly as possible, but only on Zulu soil.

Lt-Gen Lord Chelmsford, the senior British commander, is shown here in an eyewitness sketch drawn on the eve of the final battle at Ulundi. He accompanied No. 3 (Centre) Column – nominally under the command of Col Richard Glyn – at the beginning of the invasion, and it was Chelmsford's decisions that shaped the course of the iSandlwana campaign. (Ron Sheeley Collection)

MAP KEY

1 December 1878: The British invasion force assembles on the Zulu borders in five columns. Durnford's No. 2 Column and Rowlands' No. 5 Column are soon allocated a defensive role.

2 6 January 1879: Wood's No. 4 (Left Flank) Column crosses the Ncome River into disputed territory.

3 11 January 1879: Glyn's No. 3 (Centre) Column (accompanied and effectively commanded by Chelmsford) crosses into Zulu territory following the expiry of the British ultimatum.

4 12 January 1879: Pearson's No. 1 (Right Flank) Column begins to cross into Zulu territory.

5 12 January 1879: Glyn's No. 3 (Centre) Column attacks and destroys the homestead of the border chief Sihayo kaXongo.

6 17 January 1879: King Cetshwayo's *amabutho* march out from the complex of royal homesteads at oNdini.

7 18 January 1879: Cetshwayo's force divides: the main section, under Ntshingwayo kaMahole and Mavumengwana kaNdlela, strikes west towards Rorke's Drift, while a smaller detachment under Godide kaNdlela moves south to support Zulu elements harassing Pearson's advance.

8 20/21 January 1879: Durnford's No. 2 Column crosses into Zululand at Rorke's Drift to support Glyn's No. 3 (Centre) Column.

9 Mid-morning, 22 January 1879: Godide intercepts Pearson's column at Nyezane, but is driven off.

10 Early afternoon, 22 January 1879: Ntshingwayo's *amabutho* attacks and overruns the British camp at iSandlwana, destroying a significant portion of both Durnford's No. 2 and Glyn's No. 3 (Centre) Column.

11 Afternoon, 22 January 1879: The Zulu reserve under Prince Dabulamanzi kaMpande commences its assault on the British supply depot at Rorke's Drift, but fails to capture it.

12 Mid-morning, 23 January 1879: Lord Chelmsford returns to Natal with the remnants of No. 3 (Centre) Column; the exhausted *amabutho* disperse to recover, allowing the British a two-month respite during which reinforcements are hurried to southern Africa.

13 Late morning, 23 January 1879: Pearson occupies the deserted mission station at Eshowe; his force is steadily invested by the Zulu in the coming days.

14 31 January 1879: Wood moves camp to a more defensible position on Khambula Hill; from here he wages a low-intensity war directed against local Zulu loyalists.

15 12 March 1879: Zulu forces led by Mbilini waMswati attack and overrun a supply convoy of the 80th Regiment on the Ntombe River.

16 24 March 1879: Having reassembled his army, King Cetshwayo sends it north to neutralize the threat posed by Wood.

17 28 March 1879: Wood leads a mounted foray against Hlobane Mountain, but the attack goes badly and the arrival of the king's *amabutho* turns it into a British rout.

18 Morning, 29 March 1879: Chelmsford crosses the Lower Thukela River with a column of reinforcements.

19 Afternoon, 29 March 1879: Zulu forces led by Mnyamana kaNgqengelele Buthelezi attack Wood's base at Khambula in a battle directed by Ntshingwayo kaMahole but, despite hours of determined attacks, are heavily defeated.

20 2 April 1879: Chelmsford breaks the Zulu cordon around Eshowe at Gingindlovu.

21 4 April 1879: Chelmsford commences his withdrawal to the Thukela River.

22 4 April 1879: Pearson starts to withdraw to the Thukela.

23 15 April 1879: Chelmsford begins to reorganize his forces. The No. 1 (Right Flank) and Eshowe Relief columns are formed into the 1st Division, which occupies the coastal districts; a new column formed from reinforcements, the 2nd Division under Maj Gen E. Newdigate, is assembled at Landman's Drift, while Wood's No. 4 (Left Flank) Column is redesignated the Flying Column.

24 20 May 1879: British border garrisons raid across the Thukela River, provoking a Zulu counter-raid on 25 June.

25 1 June 1879: The 2nd Division, accompanied by Chelmsford himself, crosses into Zululand on 1 June; the Prince Imperial of France is killed when a 2nd Division scouting party is ambushed.

26 3 June 1879: The Flying Column joins the 2nd Division at the Tshotshosi River and the two advance in tandem.

27 24 June 1879: King Cetshwayo assembles his army once more, at oNdini.

28 4 July 1879: The combined 2nd Division and Flying Column inflict a final defeat on the *amabutho* at Ulundi. Chelmsford resigns his command on 9 July and leaves mopping-up operations to his successor, Sir Garnet Wolseley.

29 28 August 1879: King Cetshwayo is captured by elements of the 1st (King's) Dragoon Guards in the remote Ngome Forest.

30 5 September 1879: The final shots of the war are fired when local Zulu elements living near the Ntombe battlefield are suppressed by troops commanded by Col Baker Russell.

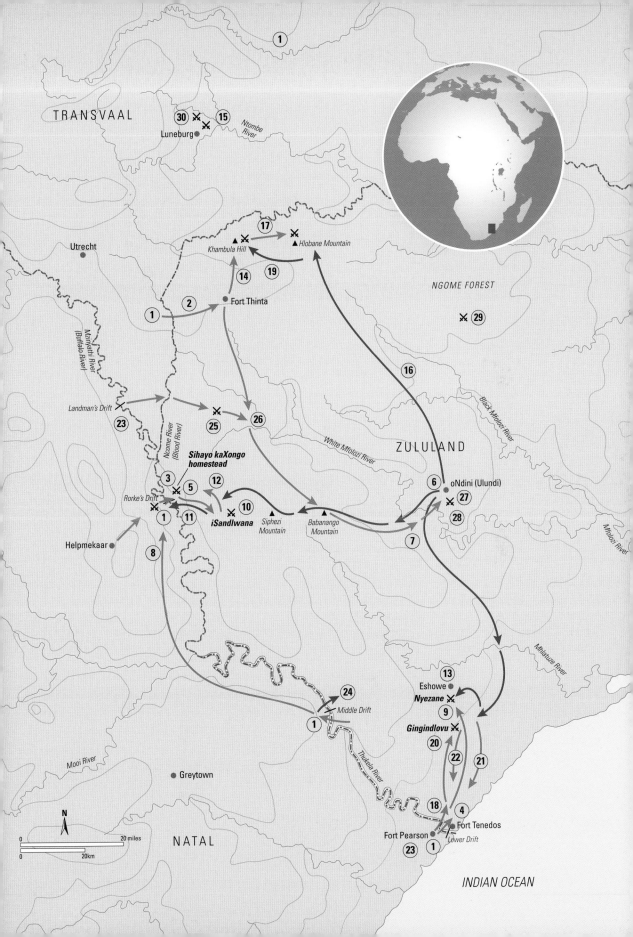

TRANSVAAL

Utrecht

Luneburg

30 ✕✕ **15**

Ntombe River

17

Khambula Hill ▲ ✕✕ ▲ Hlobane Mountain

14 **19**

2 Fort Thinta

1

*Mzinyathi River
(Buffalo River)*

Landman's Drift ✕

23

*Ncome River
(Blood River)*

✕✕ **25** **26**

3 ✕✕ **5** **12**

Rorke's Drift ✕✕

1 **11**

iSandlwana ✕✕ **10**

Helpmekaar

8

*Sihayo kaXongo
homestead*

*Siphezi
Mountain* ▲

▲ *Babanango
Mountain*

7

NGOME FOREST

ZULULAND

✕✕ **29**

White Mfolozi River

16

Black Mfolozi River

oNdini (Ulundi)

6 ✕✕ **27**

28

Mfolozi River

Mhlatuze River

13

Eshowe

Nyezane ✕✕

9

Gingindlovu ✕✕

20

22 **21**

24

Middle Drift ✕

1

Thukela River

Mooi River

Greytown

N

0 _____ 20 miles

0 _____ 20km

NATAL

18

4

Fort Tenedos

Fort Pearson

Lower Drift

23 **1**

INDIAN OCEAN

The Opposing Sides

ORIGINS AND RECRUITMENT

British

Despite a growing self-confidence in Britain's Imperial role, public attitudes towards service in the British Army and the Royal Navy – which inevitably found themselves at the sharp end of Britain's international ambitions – were entirely divided along class lines. For the gentry who provided the bulk of the Army's officers, service was regarded as one of only a few genuinely honourable employments, and was considered a valid career option for second and third sons who were unlikely to inherit family property but who did not fancy the life of a clergyman and who shared the common disdain for trade. A successful Army career could offer the hope of preferment, promotion and recognition, as well as a touch of glamour and dash to impress the ladies and to offset the risks of death or disablement in a far-away place.

For the lower sectors of society, however, from whom the ordinary soldiers or 'other ranks' were drawn, 'going for a soldier' was held in contempt. It was generally believed that enlistment in the Army was the last resort of the drunken, the degenerate and the degraded. Alcohol was a major contributing factor in individual decisions to enlist, and experienced recruiting sergeants – who were paid a bonus for each recruit they secured – were wise enough to target public houses deliberately. Yet enlistment was not without its attractions. For most it offered a roof, clothing on their backs, and three square meals a day and, if the food was monotonous – a ration of bread or biscuit, boiled meat and vegetables where available – it was often better than even those civilians regularly in employment could obtain. Pay, promised at 1 shilling a day, was lower than civilian labourers might earn, but was at least regular. Nevertheless, for some Army service simply offered an alternative to civilian life, a chance, perhaps, to escape –

from crime or punishment, from a romantic entanglement, or simply from a life without prospects or hope.

In the early Victorian Army a recruit enlisted for 12 years' continual service, with an option to re-enlist for a further 12. In an effort to attract a better class of recruit, the Army Enlistment Act of 1870 reduced the period of active service to six years, to be followed by six further years with the newly created Reserve. Certainly by the time of the Anglo-Zulu War, although there were still many long-service men working their way through the system, the Line Infantry battalions were increasingly full of younger recruits.

Once committed, a recruit was sent to join his regiment. The battalion, rather than the regiment, was the standard tactical unit of the age, a self-contained administrative unit that would frame the recruit's existence and shape his sense of belonging. At full strength a field battalion consisted of a headquarters and eight companies of 100 men apiece, yet battalions on active service were usually much under-strength due to natural wastage, sickness and desertion – and it was seldom possible in any case to maintain their integrity as a fighting unit, since individual companies were routinely detached for garrison or escort duties.

Once he had learned the basics of drill – how to stand, march and handle his rifle – the recruit was taught how to manoeuvre alongside his comrades and initiated into a life of repetitive routine. Great emphasis was placed in Army life on discipline so that a recruit learned to obey orders without question and respond automatically. Breaches of discipline, from minor issues regarding dirty or missing kit to serious offences like striking an officer or sleeping on duty, might be punished harshly, although by 1879 flogging had been abolished for peacetime service. It was, however, still applicable on active service.

The raw material of the Zulu army – a young *insizwa*, or unmarried man. Such men bore the burden of service in the royal *amabutho*, a part-time citizen militia that constituted the Zulu king's labour-gang, police force and army. This man wears typical everyday dress, and carries two impressive long-bladed stabbing-spears. (Author's Collection)

Zulu

Unlike its British counterpart, service in the Zulu military system was theoretically universal, but by no means full-time. Traditionally, Zulu men had been required to give service to their chiefs through enrolment in guilds known as *amabutho* (sing. *ibutho*), but with the inclusion of chiefdoms in the kingdom the right to raise *amabutho* passed to the king himself. Direct control of the nation's manpower was, therefore, taken out of local hands and the *amabutho* were a powerful tool of state control and royal authority.

Amabutho were formed according to the common age of their members. Every few years, depending on the population levels the king would direct that a new *ibutho* be assembled and all those youths who had reached military age – 17 or 18 – since the last call-up would be called together. Most youths looked forward to enrolment in an *ibutho* because it marked a step up in social standing and a benchmark on their journey towards adulthood.

Each *ibutho* was divided into two wings and further sub-divided into companies. There was no fixed size to an *ibutho*, nor indeed to companies, each of which might vary in strength between 50 and 80 men. While an *ibutho* would contain men from all across the country, individual companies tended to be composed of men from the same area who had served together as cadets. Although senior officers – the colonel in command, two wing commanders, and commanders of groups of companies – were appointed by the king from senior men outside the regiment, junior officers were picked from recruits who had shown aptitude in cadetship.

Having undergone a brief settling-in period, the men of a new *ibutho* were allowed to disperse and return to their civilian lives, subject only to the king's call-up and to the annual marshalling of the army that accompanied the national harvest ceremonies. They did not expect to serve continuously, and were seldom called together by the king for duty for more than a few months in the year.

The men of a particular *ibutho* were bound together by an intense *esprit de corps* that would last throughout their lives, and it was common for old men to be addressed simply by the name of their *ibutho*. Nevertheless, the burden of duty fell more heavily upon the young, since these had only limited responsibilities within wider society, and were considered to be directly under royal command. Once the men married, however, they were considered the king's to command only under special circumstances, and were seldom called upon to perform routine household duties. Because of this, successive Zulu kings had taken to themselves the right to grant permission for men to marry, and they delayed this as long as possible in order to maximize the time *amabutho* were available to serve them. Once married, an *ibutho* was usually only summoned to participate in national ceremonies, or to take part in a major war.

MOTIVATION, MORALE AND LOGISTICS

British

Although huge gulfs separated them, officers and men were bound together by a deep common commitment to both the British Crown and the traditions of their regiment, embodied in powerful symbols – badges, uniforms and battle honours – of which the Colours (flags) were the most potent. Such was the sense of *esprit de corps* possessed by individual battalions, indeed, that brawls between men from different regiments while off-duty were a common occurrence.

Active service offered an exciting alternative to the dull routine of peacetime soldiering. When Andrew Guthrie heard on 2 January 1878 that the 90th Light Infantry was under orders to sail to the 9th Cape Frontier War, he saw immediately that 'Here was a chance to leave the girls of

Portsmouth not to be thrown away. The 90th LI was one of the smartest regiments [in] Aldershot … I told the orderly sergeant to put my name down as a volunteer for the 90th. There was 21 of our department volunteered' (quoted in Macdougall 1998: 6).

Guthrie had not troubled himself with the politics of the Frontier War, merely remarking that the 90th Light Infantry was dispatched to the Cape 'to assist in quelling some disturbance' (quoted in Macdougall 1998: 6). His corresponding lack of interest in the causes of the particular war in which he was about to fight was typical of most British professional soldiers of the period. Even officers, who as a rule were far better informed and politically literate than their men, rarely expressed an opinion, rather considering it their duty to obey the orders given to them. As George Hamilton-Browne, an adventurer who had knocked about the world before taking a commission in the auxiliaries in Zululand, noted simply: 'If you wish to know the cause of the war I must refer you to the Blue Books [official Parliamentary records] for the information. It was no business of mine and my opinion was not asked on the question' (Hamilton-Browne 1912: 112).

The logistical arrangements made by the British were determined by Chelmsford's vision for the campaign. Chelmsford's initial plan was to invade Zululand in five offensive columns; these would have to carry all their provisions, camping equipment and ammunition with them, and even a small column would therefore require a large complement of locally procured ox-wagon transport. There proved to be too little of this available to go round, and Chelmsford was forced to reduce the standing of two of his columns – Durnford's No. 2 Column at the Middle Drift on the River Thukela and Rowlands' No. 5 Column on the Transvaal border – from offensive to largely defensive.

Chelmsford intended that the backbone of each of the three offensive columns would be made up of two battalions of Regular infantry, which, he

Col Charles Pearson (seated left, in civilian dress) and officers of the 2/3rd Regiment (the Buffs), photographed on the eve of the Zulu campaign. The blue infantry-pattern patrol jackets and scarlet undress frocks worn here were typical of most infantry officers' dress in the field. Pearson was the senior officer in Natal from November 1876 to December 1877, but went on half-pay in November 1878, thereby passing command of the battalion to Lt-Col H. Parnell. Pearson was then appointed commander of No. 1 (Right Flank) Column, however, of which the Buffs were a part. Few officers below middle-rank or men in Parnell's battalion had previous combat experience, since the battalion had not seen active service since being raised in 1857. Although it had been stationed in southern Africa since 1876, it had been largely based in Natal, and had not taken part in the 9th Cape Frontier War or the Sekhukhune expedition. (National Army Museum)

A group of ORs of the 2/3rd Regiment with Zulu prisoners in April 1879. The British are wearing the loose undress frock with facing colour for this battalion on the collar tabs but not the cuffs. They are wearing their equipment braces to support the weight of full ammunition pouches but, judging from the unattached under-arm straps, are not carrying their greatcoats; nor are they wearing their haversacks or water-bottles as they would on the march. Their prisoners are neither identified nor wearing any distinctive regalia. (Author's Collection)

OPPOSITE
Most Zulu men wore little more than their everyday dress into battle, albeit carrying their regimental war-shields. This man is of the age of the uKhandempemvu, and carrying a pattern of shield associated with that *ibutho*. (Author's Collection)

hoped, would provide sufficient firepower to defeat any attack. Even if the Zulu campaign were to follow the same pattern, Chelmsford could not expect his infantry to fulfil all his needs, however, and in particular there was an acute shortage of mounted troops. After much political wrangling the Natal authorities were persuaded to place their Volunteer units – small part-time corps raised from the settler community for the colony's defence – at his disposal, and these were augmented by several units of Irregulars (full-time units raised by the Army from among the settlers for a period of fixed service). Furthermore, Chelmsford was well aware that the African population of Natal had a history of antagonism towards the Zulu Royal House, and he again persuaded the reluctant authorities to raise from among them a force of both mounted and foot auxiliaries to be known as the Natal Native Contingent.

Although the British Army remained the same structured and disciplined organization on campaign as it was in peacetime, the rigorous conditions of life in the field tended to break down some of the distance which existed between officers and other ranks at home. Officers could spend their own money procuring whatever luxuries might be available, and had a large baggage allowance to transport them, while ordinary soldiers subsisted on a basic ration often made erratic by complications in the chain of supply. Nevertheless, for the time a campaign lasted, the same sun shone on them both, and the same rain dripped through leaky canvas or ran under the bottom of tents without favour at night.

Zulu

Rivalries between *amabutho* were as commonplace as those between British infantry battalions, particularly among those who were close in age, and who therefore jockeyed for reputation. Brawls between *amabutho* were frequent and the Zulu kings had to manage their men carefully when the entire army was gathered together, although these rivalries were often channelled to good effect through pre-battle ceremonies that encouraged *amabutho* to outdo one another in action.

Pride in the nation's warrior reputation, and the sense of belonging which membership of an *ibutho* inculcated, meant that morale within the Zulu army was usually very high at the beginning of a campaign. In 1879 the prevailing mood among the *amabutho* was one of indignation at the presumption of the British. The Zulu leaders were wise enough to appreciate, however, that this heady atmosphere would leech away the longer a campaign went on, and the army functioned best when it had clearly recognizable short-term objectives; it was at its most successful when it could fight while that early enthusiasm was still at its strongest. In 1879, the presence of British columns operating on Zulu soil perfectly fulfilled that criterion.

British intelligence sources suggested that Cetshwayo could command a total of some 40,000 men. In fact, although the king was able to maintain small armies of several thousand men concurrently with his main striking army, he would never be able to put more than 25,000 men into the field on any single occasion. At the outset of a campaign the *amabutho* first assembled at their barracks, where they were issued with war-shields, and then marched to a general assembly point specified by the king, where they were ritually prepared for war. From there they set off on campaign arrayed in a single column then, when they drew near the enemy, split into two columns, screened by scouts and marching a mile or two apart to reduce the risk of being

surprised. There was no baggage train – the king simply allocated a herd of cattle to sustain the warriors for a day or two, the men brought a few supplies of cold meat and roasted corn themselves, and lads too young to have been yet enrolled carried sleeping mats, shields and food for fathers or elder brothers. Even so, allocated food supplies were usually exhausted within the

This plate depicts a soldier of the 1/24th Regiment. In January 1879 the men of the 1/24th Regiment were generally lean, tanned and fit, their martial appearance heightened by their beards, which – while prohibited for peacetime soldiering – were positively encouraged in the field. By this time life in the southern African bush had already taken its toll on their uniforms; new uniforms and kit were only issued annually, in April, and these might take months reaching troops at remote outposts, so that the majority of the British soldiers moving from the Eastern Cape Frontier to Zululand looked crumpled, experienced, and decidedly businesslike.

Weapons, dress and equipment

As a breech-loader, the Martini-Henry rifle (**1**) could easily be loaded while kneeling or lying down. Blistered fingers had taught the men that the Martini-Henry barrels became painfully hot when exposed ordinarily to the African sun, and more so after firing rounds in action, and many men had sewn a leather collar (**2**) around the stock to protect their left hands. For close-quarter fighting other ranks were issued with a triangular-section socket bayonet (**3**), while sergeants were equipped with a heavier sword bayonet.

The white foreign-service helmet (**4**) as issued had proved an obvious target to enemy riflemen, and the brass regimental plates had long since been removed and the helmets dulled with dyes improvised from tea, coffee or boiled bark. Line regiments (other than

Rifles) still wore red coats (**5**) on active service, but after some time on campaign the five-button undress frocks that were standard issue for field use were torn and patched, often with makeshift colours, and so too were the trousers (**6**). The heavy valise was usually carried on regimental transport wagons, but troops on the march still carried their greatcoats and mess-tin – although these were usually left behind when defending a camp. Sometimes men retained the equipment braces but often, as shown here, they fought simply in belts (**7**), pouches, each of which held two packets of ten rounds (**8**), water-bottle (**9**) and haversack (**10**). The black 'expense pouch' (**11**) – which carried 30 loose rounds – was usually worn in front of the right hip, where it could easily be reached when loading and firing.

first two or three days and the *amabutho* survived thereafter by foraging. This was difficult in 1879 since, as they were fighting on Zulu soil, they in effect had to carry away the food supplies of the very people they were supposed to be protecting. As a result, it was not unusual for the *amabutho* to go into battle hungry.

Although the distances covered by a Zulu *impi* – a blanket term meaning an armed force – on the march have been exaggerated, an *ibutho* could easily cover 20 miles a day. Accustomed to walking long distances across rocky hillsides in bare feet in their daily lives, to crossing rivers or picking their way through the bush, the warriors saw no extra challenge in traversing the countryside while on campaign.

LEADERSHIP

British

Officers who were only seen across the length of the parade ground in peacetime became a familiar sight on campaign in the regimental village formed each night by the battalion camp. Soldiers became more accustomed to working under their company officers – a captain and two lieutenants – and even the colonel commanding the battalion became a less remote figure. Nevertheless, for most private soldiers, the most conspicuous figures of authority remained their company NCOs, with whom the responsibility remained of ensuring the smooth transmission of orders from above and the practical day-to-day management of the battalion.

NCOs were promoted from the ranks, and any soldier proved capable, diligent and sober might aspire one day to be appointed corporal, the first step

Evelyn Wood, centre, and his staff officers photographed towards the end of the war. Wood was an able and determined officer whose reputation, even so, owed much to his political skill at stressing his victories and obscuring the failings that led to his occasional defeats. Although the Staff College had existed in various forms since 1802 to train Army officers in staff duties, no independent staff body existed in 1879 and staff appointments were made by commanding officers from applicants among regimental or special service officers. Although by the 1870s many ambitious officers recognized the professional advantages of passing the Staff College courses, rank, regimental affiliations and personal connections all continued to have a major influence on such appointments in the field. (Author's Collection)

Officers of the 90th Light Infantry with Wood's No. 4 (Left Flank) Column. These were the men who led the battalion at Khambula on 29 March 1879. British infantry and cavalry officers were trained in their professional duties at the Royal Military College, Sandhurst, and by 1879 the 90th Light Infantry was a relatively experienced battalion. The commanding officer, Bvt-Col R.M. Rogers, was a veteran of the Crimean War and the 2nd Anglo-Chinese War (1856–60), where he had won the Victoria Cross; although the battalion had contained a high proportion of short-service recruits when it arrived in southern Africa in 1878, it had served throughout the closing stages of the 9th Cape Frontier War before taking part in the invasion of Zululand. Although none of the officers is wearing his weapons in this photograph, in battle each would have carried a sword and a revolver. (Author's Collection)

in a progression that might eventually see him rise to the exalted heights of colour sergeant or sergeant major. Nevertheless, so rigid were the class distinctions within the Army that there were almost no routes by which an NCO might progress upwards to become an officer, and inevitably sergeants of many years' standing were still under the authority of young lieutenants with little or no experience. It was a wise junior officer, then, who learned to recognize something of his own limitations, and to appreciate the practical experience of the NCOs of his company.

In battle, orders within a battalion were passed verbally where possible, or by written order where distances were too great, from the colonel in command to company officers. Company officers directed the deployment of their men, with the senior NCOs supervising the placement. Since words of command were often drowned by the din in companies actually engaged, the instruction manual dictated that commands then should be executed by bugle-calls.

Zulu

It was the practice to appoint junior officers from within the ranks of a newly enrolled *ibutho*. The young men had been under scrutiny from the time they had first been summoned to cadetship, and those who had displayed a natural talent for leadership had been noted. The more senior officers, however, were always appointed by the king and his council from outsiders, from older, more experienced men. These would include the *induna'nkhulu*, the 'great *induna*', who was effectively the *ibutho*'s colonel, and at least two subordinates, who commanded a wing each. It was quite common, too, particularly in a larger *ibutho* like the uKhandempemvu, to appoint intermediate officers, each of whom commanded a division of companies. All these outside appointees

This plate depicts a warrior of the uKhandempemvu *ibutho* as he would have appeared at iSandlwana. This *ibutho* – which was also known as the uMcijo – consisted of men around the age of 30.

Weapons, dress and equipment

The men took their personal weapons to war; those with firearms carried their rough shot and unreliable powder in whatever manner of pouches or powder-horns they had managed to procure from white traders. In the early days of the kingdom a big shield, which measured some 50in tall and 30in wide and was called *isihlangu*, was the norm but in the 1850s Cetshwayo had introduced a smaller variant, the *umbhumbhuluzo* (**1**), which was about 40in by 20in, and which had achieved considerable popularity as being both lighter and easier to wield. The uKhandempemvu *ibutho* carried several different patterns: either brown shields with a large white spot on the left side, black shields with broken bands of white at the top and bottom, or white shields with a broad black band across the centre.

Although every *ibutho* possessed a distinctive ceremonial uniform of fine feathers and furs, worn to important national occasions, many of the pelts were too rare and fragile to risk in the rigorous conditions of campaign life. When King Cetshwayo summoned his army

in January 1879 most men simply attended wearing their daily costume – a thin belt of hide (**2**) with a curtain of tails known as an *isinene* (**3**), made up of twisted strips of fur, at the front, and a small square of calf-skin, *ibeshu* (**4**), at the back. A few wore ornaments made of cow-tail streamers, stitched to leather thongs, and tied either above the elbows or below the knees, while some wore a lighter version of the heavy cow-tail necklaces that were such a feature of ceremonial costume.

For the most part the more conservative, senior men seem to have retained more regalia in action than the young men while *izinduna*, officers, could generally be recognized by items with connotations of authority, such as a single Blue Crane feather upright at the front of the headdress, or a small bunch of crimson and green lourie feathers at the side or back of the head. Most men wore necklaces (**5**) containing ritual medicines in small pouches of animal-skin or gourds designed to protect them from harm.

The Zulu general Ntshingwayo kaMahole, who commanded during both the iSandlwana and Khambula campaigns, was reluctant to allow himself to be photographed, although this study is generally accepted to be him (seated, with rifle). (Author's Collection)

were senior men, drawn from married *amabutho*, who had both the status and natural authority to properly exercise command.

Although young Zulu men were accustomed from childhood to the authority of their elders, the *amabutho* were notoriously boisterous when assembled together and it took considerable natural ability to control them. Zulu officers were not averse to exercising their ability with the stick, however, and even in battle they might try to direct or restrain their men by striking at the shields or even heads of those who stepped too far out of line. The commanders of the *amabutho* accompanied their men into battle, exhorting them by personal example, and by 1879 many of them had acquired horses from European traders, which made them both more conspicuous and mobile. All orders were delivered verbally – by shouting over the din of battle – although high-pitched whistles were used to direct and encourage small groups of men in the immediate vicinity, and sometimes a shield might be held up to direct a particular movement.

Zulu commanders traditionally took up a position on high ground behind an assault, preferably one which gave them a commanding overview. They were accompanied by a staff drawn from the various *amabutho* who could advise or serve as messengers to carry orders as the battle developed. Generally, however, once an assault had begun it took on a momentum of its own, which was difficult to control by verbal messages carried by runners alone, and the movement of particular *amabutho* within an attack was left to the initiative of their individual commanders: while the overall plan was clearly understood, it was left to these men to exploit local enemy weaknesses or to choose the correct moment for an attack.

It was often difficult to amend elements within an attack once it had begun, due to the exuberance of the *amabutho* and to the distances involved, although if necessary a commander might send a runner from among his staff with fresh orders. This famously happened at the battle of iSandlwana when the uKhandempemvu were pinned down under British rifle fire; the commanding general, Ntshingwayo kaMahole, spotted this and sent one of his staff, chief Mkhosana kaMvundlana – who was an appointed officer of the uKhandempemvu – to urge them on. The uKhandempemvu then renewed their attack, and the incident marked a turning point in the battle.

ARMAMENT, TRAINING AND TACTICS

British

In the 1870s, British tactical theory was beginning to shift away from the practices that had been enshrined by Britain's defeat of Napoleon at the beginning of the century. While infantry manuals still advocated the advantages of marching in column but deploying in line to attack, there were significant concessions to the growing awareness of the impact improved firepower had had upon the battlefield.

The standard infantry arm was the Martini-Henry rifle, first issued in 1874, a robust and accurate single-shot breech-loader sighted up to 1,000yd – although only a select few could expect practical results on even massed targets at such a range, and its most effective battlefield range was at 400yd or less. The Martini-Henry's heavy charge produced a thumping recoil that grew worse with extended use as the mechanism became fouled with discharge residues. The retractor sometimes tore the end off the thin brass of the Boxer cartridge after a shot, particularly when the breech was hot from firing, leaving the firer to try to push out the debris by passing the cleaning rod down the barrel. Even so, the weapon was popular among the troops, who placed great faith in its abilities.

Perhaps the most accurate image of a Zulu attack to emerge from the war, sketched by the war artist Charles Fripp, who witnessed it at Ulundi. An advancing *ibutho* (behind) deploys into line of companies as it first comes under British artillery fire. The men themselves are of a young, unmarried age-group, and carry a mix of traditional weapons and firearms, but are led by an older married *induna* (foreground), who carries a status weapon, an *isizenze* (axe), denoting his authority. (Author's Collection)

The standard British infantry weapon of the late 1870s – the single-shot breech-loading Martini-Henry rifle. The breech is opened by depressing the lever and the heavy .450 cartridge inserted at the top; after firing, the lever again ejects the spent cartridge. Robust and accurate, the Martini-Henry was generally reliable, although the soft brass of the cartridges sometimes tore when the weapon was hot from heavy action, causing jamming. (Author's Collection)

Tactical doctrine recognized the merits of both massed volley fire and independent fire – volley fire was easier to control and more effective physically and psychologically against targets en masse, while independent fire was potentially individually more accurate but difficult to control – but stressed the importance of slow, measured firing. In the excitement of combat it was all too easy for men to blaze away quickly without taking proper aim, while the propellant of the Boxer cartridges fired by the Martini-Henry produced a thin cough of white smoke which could easily build, on a windless day and with hundreds of men firing, to a dense cloud that obscured the target.

Until 1877 a battalion was expected to advance deployed in line in close order, screened by skirmishers, but the new Field Exercise Manual of that year advocated instead the principle of attacks developing in depth. Two companies were to be deployed in extended order with two more behind them in support and the remainder of the battalion (four companies) further back still as a reserve. The two leading companies were to push forward, firing as they went, until they formed a single line, backed up by their supports, and fed by the reserve as necessary; once they had achieved fire superiority over their enemy a final rush might be made with the bayonet.

Two men of the 1/24th Regiment, showing something of the effects of prolonged campaigning on the Eastern Cape Frontier. Helmets are battered or replaced by civilian hats, uniforms are heavily patched, and one man wears civilian trousers. Note the cow-hide cover stitched over the stock of the rifle to protect the fingers against a barrel routinely made uncomfortable to touch by the hot African sun. (Author's Collection)

When skirmishing in extended order a company would form two lines, the men 3 paces (7½ft) apart – or more, at the discretion of the commanding officer – and usually kneeling, the rear rank rising to pass through the front before taking

up a new firing position. In a massed battalion attack, men were not expected to take cover for fear of disrupting the manoeuvre, but in general skirmishing they were allowed to do so where appropriate.

The essential elements of these manoeuvres – of forming, deploying, extending, changing front or re-forming – were a major part of British infantry drill. The British Army still placed great faith in the moral effect of the bayonet on the battlefield and recruits were taught a full range of bayonet-fighting techniques, although practical musketry instruction was constrained by strict limits on the number of available rounds. Although 200 rounds were allocated annually per man for training purposes, many battalions were reluctant to expend so many, and many recent recruits were shipped to the latter stages of the Zulu campaign having only ever fired a handful of rounds in practice.

On the eve of the invasion of Zululand, Lord Chelmsford issued instructions to his column commanders on the formations in which he preferred them to fight. These were based on techniques which had proved successful on the Eastern Cape, where experience suggested that an extended firing line of regular infantry could provide a curtain of fire which – providing the flanks were adequately protected – the Xhosa had proved unable to penetrate. Chelmsford's instructions for Zululand were that his regular infantry should similarly deploy in line, supported where possible by artillery pieces in the centre, and by auxiliary troops at an angle on either side so as to refuse the flanks. The prevailing opinion was that greater intervals between files than those prescribed in the manuals would not pose any undue risk.

A photograph summing up the disparity in military technology that would assure British victory. It shows the two Gatling guns of No. 10 Battery, 7th Brigade, Royal Artillery, which took part in the battle of Ulundi, commanded by Maj Owen, left. Although these guns were prone to jamming, their effect – when they worked – on the Zulu rushes at close range would be devastating. (Author's Collection)

Capt Glennie and men of the 2/24th Regiment, photographed towards the end of the war. They appear to be wearing light marching order and, while beards were prohibited for peace-time service, they were generally permitted or even encouraged in the field. Most battalions dyed their white foreign-service helmets to make them less conspicuous but some, including the 2/24th Regiment, seem to have preferred to improvise protective canvas covers instead. (Author's Collection)

Zulu

When ordered to assemble in January 1879 the *amabutho* did so ready for war. They left their homes for the muster without wearing the complex finery they wore on ceremonial occasions but carrying their personal weapons. These consisted of the short, broad-bladed stabbing spears which had been such an iconic part of both the practice and psychology of Zulu warfare since the foundation of the kingdom, 50 years before. Many also carried a few lighter throwing spears and perhaps a polished stick with a round head, which served as a club. Many, too, took firearms, for guns had been much sought after from European traders for decades. The exact numbers of guns available to the Zulu in 1879 can only be estimated, but some contemporary British reports place it at upwards of 20,000, and even this might be an underestimate.

Generally, however, guns were a luxury commodity, much more readily available to men of established means, and less so to the young men of the most active *amabutho*. In reviewing the *amabutho* on the eve of war King Cetshwayo had noted that the youngest *ibutho*, the uVe, was woefully short of guns, and had directed that supplies be hurriedly bought to equip them. Even where there were sufficient firearms to go round, the quality remained poor, for most were outmoded patterns dumped cheaply on the international market once they had become obsolete among the world powers. While many were muzzle-loading Enfield percussion types, or their equivalent, there were still many thousands of older flintlock Brown Bess muskets in Zululand. Good-quality powder was in short supply, as were bullets, and ammunition was usually carried in old belts or pouches sold by the traders or improvised by the men themselves.

A few Zulu had been trained to use guns effectively by the professional hunting parties that operated in Zululand from the 1850s, but most had not, and had only the haziest idea of how to get the best results from their weapons. As a result of these factors, observers noted that Zulu musketry was often heavy in battle – but very little of it was accurate. Many Zulu, indeed, regarded a gun as merely an extension of their throwing spears, and rather than engage in prolonged fire-fights they preferred to advance as close as possible to the enemy, fire a shot and then throw down their firearm, and rush forward with their stabbing spears.

Before engaging in a battle it was usual for the *amabutho* to be drawn up in a circle where they were spattered with protective medicines, intended to stiffen their resolve and ward off harm, and given a few stirring words by their commanders who encouraged them to live up to the traditions of their past kings. They were then usually deployed in an encircling formation known as *izimpondo zankomo*, the 'beasts' horns', which had been a favourite tactic since the founding of the kingdom. The youngest, most agile and eager *amabutho* were deployed on either flank as 'horns', who rushed out to surround the enemy, while older, more experienced *amabutho* were deployed in the centre, the 'chest'. The 'chest' was expected to withstand the casualties that might be expected from making a frontal assault in the open. A reserve, usually composed of older, married *amabutho*, perhaps supported by cadets not yet fully enrolled, was kept back, ready to be fed forward where necessary. Positions within this formation were jealously guarded, and may even have been specified in the royal council before the army marched out.

As the *amabutho* moved off to attack they extended into loose, open lines, allowing each man plenty of room to move freely with his shield and weapons, and to minimize the danger of presenting a compact target. The *amabutho* often broke into chants recalling past glories as they advanced, or called out regimental or national war-cries – the national war-cry in 1879 was '*uSuthu!*' – to encourage themselves, and the sight of one *ibutho* excelling in an attack was usually enough to produce a rush among the others. The advance was screened by skirmishers made up from each regiment, men who were known to show initiative, aggression and courage, and these skirmishers were thrown far ahead of the main body and, making what use of the ground they could, to attack and drive back any enemy scouts or small parties of they encountered. Only as the

The matter of which items of costume to retain in battle was a matter of personal choice and some, like this youth, undoubtedly wore a few plumes or other items associated with their *ibutho*. This man is of a younger age group and carried a plain dark shield of the smaller *umbhumbhuluzo* regimental type. (Author's Collection)

For the most part the Zulu army remained committed to its traditional close-quarter weapons, and in particular the broad-bladed stabbing spear (*iklwa*) shown in the centre here, and the wooden club, (*iwisa*). The shield (white with small red/brown patches) is of the colour associated with the senior uThulwana *ibutho*, which fought at Rorke's Drift and elsewhere. (Author's Collection)

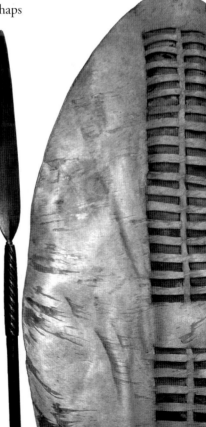

By 1879 the Zulu army was equipped with thousands of firearms although most, like this French model from the 1840s, were outmoded percussion – or even flintlock – patterns dumped on the world market by European suppliers once they became obsolete. They were often sold with inferior-quality powder and rough or home-made projectiles, none of which improved their accuracy or aim. This particular example has, none the less, been decorated by an appreciative owner with typical Zulu wire-work and brass studs. (Author's Collection)

RIGHT
The basis of most male Zulu dress was a thin belt with an apron of tails, called an *isinene*, in front and a small square of soft cow-hide, *ibeshu*, over the buttocks. This is a typical *isinene*, each tail being made from strips of fur carefully twisted around a central core. Men of rank might wear an *isinene* made from strips of spotted-cat fur, such as serval, and an *ibeshu* of leopard-skin. (Author's Collection)

FAR RIGHT
Two war-shields from 1879 displaying the difference in sizes between the *umbhumbhuluzo* pattern (left) and the older *isihlangu* type. The colours are of the iNgobamakhosi (left) and uKhandempemvu. (Author's Collection)

army surrounded the enemy, and the 'horns of the beast' closed in, did the contracting front mean that the loose lines became massed ready for the final assault.

The *izimpondo zankomo* formation was designed to play to the Zulu army's traditional strengths – to bring the maximum number of men into close combat as quickly as possible. Once they reached the enemy, the warriors relied on a practised dexterity with their weapons, hurling their throwing spears at a range of 10–20yd, then drawing their stabbing spears. The shield was not merely used for defensive purposes but also to batter an enemy, knocking him off-guard and exposing him to an under-arm thrust at the chest or stomach with the stabbing spear. This final rush usually produced a surge of elation among the warriors, resulting in a ferocious attack that was difficult, without the protection of barricades, to repulse.

If a Zulu attack managed to strike home it usually resulted in victory in battle. The trick, as the British came to realize after the early defeats of 1879, was to prevent them from doing so, and the battles which followed developed a familiar pattern in which one side attacked and sought to close – while the other did their best to shoot them down before they did so.

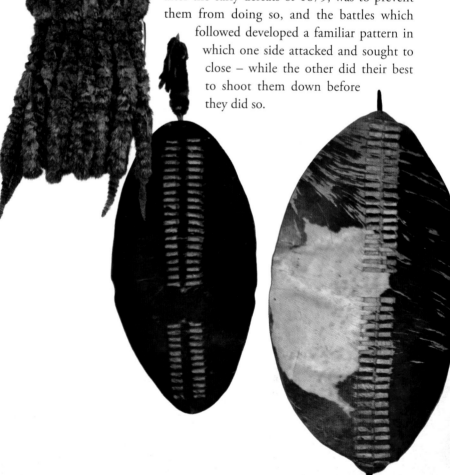

Nyezane

22 January 1879

BACKGROUND TO BATTLE

The five British columns crossed into Zululand when the ultimatum expired on 11 January 1879, and the following day elements of No. 3 (Centre) Column, accompanied by Chelmsford himself, attacked the homestead of an important border chieftain living opposite Rorke's Drift. The implication was not lost at oNdini, and on 17 January the fully prepared Zulu army set out for the front. The following day, 3,000 or 4,000 men split away to march towards the coast to join the forces gathered to oppose Col Pearson's No. 1 (Right Flank) Column, the rest – perhaps 25,000 strong, and swollen along the way by late-comers who had missed the general muster – marching straight towards Rorke's Drift.

In the weeks preceding the expiry of the British ultimatum on 11 January 1879 the weather had made life uncomfortable for Pearson's force, camped on

Invasion – a company of the 99th Regiment crosses into Zululand by pont at the Lower Drift of the Thukela River. Newcomers to southern Africa, the men are still wearing their brass helmet-plates on their white helmets; later these would be removed and the helmets stained a less conspicuous neutral shade with dyes made from tea or coffee. They are also wearing the earlier-issue undress frock with a single loop of braid on the cuff rather than the later pattern with trefoil cuff design. (Author's Collection)

Zulu warriors lie in wait for Pearson's approaching column on the march to Eshowe. Despite the rather dramatic style favoured by the down-market illustrated press in the UK – and the presence of too much regalia among the Zulu – the picture nevertheless captures something of the initial encounter at Nyezane. (Author's Collection)

the Natal bank of the Thukela River. It had taken Pearson several days to ferry his column across the river but the crossing was not opposed and by 16 January he had established a large, sprawling camp on the Zulu bank and begun work on an earthwork, named Fort Tenedos, to protect it.

Pearson's orders were to advance on oNdini, but first to occupy a Norwegian mission station, Eshowe, which lay 35 miles by road from the Thukela. The mission had been abandoned before the war began, but in a country where there were few permanent structures Lord Chelmsford had identified it as a potential supply depot on the road to oNdini, and Pearson was to establish himself there pending coordination with the advance of the other two columns.

Progress over the first few days was slow. The passage of so many wagons over the old traders' track had such a detrimental effect that Pearson had decided to advance in two divisions in the hope that the road might dry out between them. He had a total of 4,271 combat troops at his disposal, including all eight companies of the 2/3rd Regiment, 'The Buffs', which, despite having been in Africa since 1876, were nearly at full strength at 749 officers and men. He also had six companies of the 99th Regiment – also close to full strength at 515 men – who had only arrived fresh from England a few days before; Lt Julius Batt Backhouse of the Buffs thought the 99th 'a very young lot of men' (quoted in Castle & Knight 1994: 39).

The countryside appeared deserted apart from a few scouts captured by Pearson's patrols, one of whom admitted that they were local men who had not joined their *amabutho* for the muster at oNdini but had been directed by the king to remain in the area to watch the British movements. In fact, unknown to Pearson, Cetshwayo had ordered them to be reinforced by a detachment of the men gathered at oNdini. These were under the command of Godide kaNdlela and consisted of about 40 companies of the uMxapho *ibutho* – about 2,600 men in all – and a further 15 companies of the uDlambedlu and izinGulube *amabutho*, some 900 men. The uMxapho were still young men, in their mid-30s and unmarried, but the uDlambedlu and izinGulube were in their 50s.

Godide's plan seems to have been to occupy the kwaGingindlovu royal homestead, which lay between Pearson and Eshowe, and there rendezvous with the local elements watching the British advance. In fact, however, Pearson – whose scouts had begun to report rumours of a Zulu presence in the area – reached kwaGingindlovu first, on 21 January, and found it deserted. His men set it on fire before advancing a few miles to a position closer to the Nyezane River, where they spent the night. Godide's men arrived at kwaGingindlovu that evening to find it a smouldering ruin and quickly moved to intercept Pearson at his new campsite. Some elements of the *amabutho* approached the British camp that night under cover of darkness but the sound of British sentries calling out convinced them that the British were on the alert and Godide decided instead to retire to the cover of a range of hills that blocked the track closer to Eshowe.

INTO COMBAT

Reveille was sounded in the British camp at 0330hrs on the 22nd, but despite evidence of movement in the flattened grass Pearson decided to press on. The Nyezane lay just a few miles ahead, and on the far side the hills rose up steeply. The river itself was narrow but the banks were steep and it was full after the recent rain; it offered such an obvious point of ambush that Pearson sent his mounted men ahead to investigate it. They returned to report no sign of a Zulu presence, and Pearson instructed his First Division to cross the river, ordering the men and wagons to rest on a grassy space at the foot of the hills on the far side while the rest were brought across. Welman's Second Division started a few hours after the first with the intention of crossing the river once the first had moved on.

Shortly after 0800hrs, however, a small party of Zulu was seen on the hills further up the track and Pearson sent forward a company of the 1/2nd NNC to clear them away, under the personal command of a Regular officer, Capt Arthur Fitzroy Hart, who was attached to them as staff officer. The Zulu dropped off the track to the British right, passing through a narrow valley choked with bush and emerging onto the flank of a steeper hill, known to the Zulu as Wombane, beyond. The NNC company followed them. The Zulu moved off Wombane and onto the next rise, but then disappeared. As they pushed up the slope in the long grass after them, some of the NNC became aware of a faint buzzing sound ahead of them and tried to attract the attention of their officers, but to no avail. They had gone only a little further when, according to Hart,

MAP KEY

1 0100hrs (approx.): The main Zulu force camps beyond the crest of Wombane Hill, out of sight of the British column.

2 0800hrs (approx.): Having previously scouted the heights opposite, the First Division of Pearson's Column begins to cross the Nyezane River. Wagons are parked on a flat to the left of the road as they cross.

3 0805hrs (approx.): A party of Zulu scouts on the slopes of Wombane Hill are spotted by the British, and Capt Hart's company of the 1/2nd NNC is sent forward to drive them off.

4 0815hrs (approx.): Hart's men blunder into scouts from the uMxapho *ibutho* concealed in the grass. The Zulu open fire and pursue the NNC back towards the road.

5 0820hrs (approx.): The rest of the uMxapho rush forward and extend as a left 'horn', streaming down Wombane in an attempt to surround the British.

6 0820hrs (approx.): Pearson hurries the troops at the head of the column up the road to form a firing line on a knoll facing east-north-east towards Wombane.

7 0840hrs (approx.): Troops at the rear of the British column deploy in extended order and skirmish towards the tip of the Zulu left 'horn', preventing the ambushers from completely outflanking the column.

8 0840hrs (approx.): The attack of the Zulu right 'horn' is hesitant and is halted by a vedette (outpost) of seven men led by Sgt Preller of the Natal Hussars.

9 0900hrs (approx.): Having been hurried forward up the road, the Gatling from HMS *Active*'s Naval Brigade deploys on the knoll, firing a short burst at Zulu hidden in bush at the foot of Wombane Hill.

10 0910hrs (approx.): In response to the Zulu 'chest' flanking fire from a deserted homestead further up the road, NNC NCOs, led by Hart and supported by the Naval Brigade, mount a charge and drive the Zulu out of the homestead.

11 0920hrs (approx.): Advanced detachments from the British Second Division arrive on the battlefield and deploy to the right of the road; by this time, however, the Zulu have abandoned the attack and are retiring across the field.

Battlefield environment

In the summer of 1879 the coastal lowlands through which Pearson's command advanced were hot and humid. The jagged and jutting uplands of the mountain foothills inland gave way here to a succession of rolling downs that stretched towards the horizon, and were cut through by a succession of rivers flowing eastwards on the final stage of their journey to the Indian Ocean. Natal and Zululand had seen several years of below-average rainfall in the 1870s but at the end of 1878 the drought broke. Baking hot days gave way to fierce thunderstorms in the evenings and sudden, heavy downpours that turned the bigger rivers to raging torrents and made every minor stream an obstacle to military transport. The countryside was carpeted in long, wet green grass, and thick bush and reeds grew in profusion along the river-beds; here and there ancient forests crested the ridge-tops.

Because of its proximity to the coast, and because of the good drift across the Thukela River lying just a few miles upstream from its mouth, this area had seen more European traffic than much of the country, and indeed Cetshwayo's predecessor, King Mpande, had deliberately tried to confine the influence of European missionaries and traders to the coast. John Dunn – Cetshwayo's white adviser – lived there, and as a result the fragile membrane of wagon-tracks upon which Pearson would depend for his advance was better established there than elsewhere. A good track connected the Lower Thukela Drift to mission stations, abandoned before war broke out, on the Zulu side of the border, one of which – the Norwegian outpost at Eshowe – Chelmsford had specified as Pearson's first strategic objective.

The battlefield of Nyezane today. The winding course of the river is marked by the line of bush, left; on the morning of 22 January Pearson crossed the river, the head of his baggage train parking on the flats below the hills, waiting for the rest to come up. The track passed up through the hills on the central spur (just above the white hut); Godide's Zulu had spent the previous night beyond the high hill centre right, Wombane. The first encounter took place on the slopes of Wombane, provoking the Zulu left to mount a determined attack down the hill, attempting to outflank the column and strike at the wagons crossing the drift. (Author's Collection)

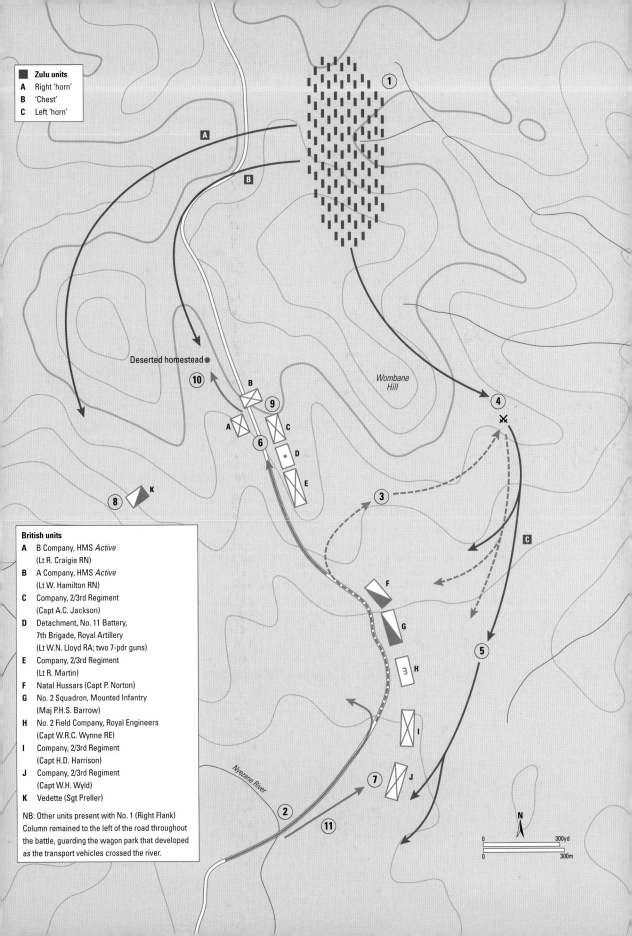

Zulu units
A Right 'horn'
B 'Chest'
C Left 'horn'

Deserted homestead

Wombane
Hill

British units
A   B Company, HMS *Active*
     (Lt R. Craigie RN)
B   A Company, HMS *Active*
     (Lt W. Hamilton RN)
C   Company, 2/3rd Regiment
     (Capt A.C. Jackson)
D   Detachment, No. 11 Battery,
     7th Brigade, Royal Artillery
     (Lt W.N. Lloyd RA; two 7-pdr guns)
E   Company, 2/3rd Regiment
     (Lt R. Martin)
F   Natal Hussars (Capt P. Norton)
G   No. 2 Squadron, Mounted Infantry
     (Maj P.H.S. Barrow)
H   No. 2 Field Company, Royal Engineers
     (Capt W.R.C. Wynne RE)
I   Company, 2/3rd Regiment
     (Capt H.D. Harrison)
J   Company, 2/3rd Regiment
     (Capt W.H. Wyld)
K   Vedette (Sgt Preller)

NB: Other units present with No. 1 (Right Flank)
Column remained to the left of the road throughout
the battle, guarding the wagon park that developed
as the transport vehicles crossed the river.

Nyezane River

N

0   300yd
0   300m

... suddenly a mass of Zulus appeared on the hilltop on our left, and opened fire of musketry upon us at a distance of about 400 yards. I saw at once that we had almost fallen into a trap, and I instantly gave the order 'Retire'. At the same moment the Zulus poured down the hill by hundreds at the top of their speed, with a tremendous shout, while others above kept up the fire over the heads of those descending the hill ... bullets whistled amongst us and struck the earth all about as we went. (Hart-Synnot 1912: 106)

Hart became separated from his men during the scamper back to the road, and later discovered that several of the European officers and NCOs of the company had tried to make a stand to cover the retreat. They were heavily outnumbered, however, and were easily overrun, and one officer, one sergeant, three corporals and three men were killed. The officer, Lt J.L. Raines, had been shot clean through the head, but the rest had all apparently been speared at close quarters. Zulu warriors passing over the bodies after they fell marked their participation in the incident by stabbing at them where they lay, so that Raines' body was, according to one Volunteer of the Stanger Mounted Rifles, 'so riddled with assegai wounds that it would have been impossible to place your hands anywhere on his body without covering one' (quoted in Castle & Knight 1994: 58).

Just as Hart reached the road he met Pearson riding up, attracted by the sound of the firing. Most elements of the First Division were now across the river, although some wagons were still waiting their turn, while the Second Division was some miles further back down the road. 'Some men of the Buffs were already up', recalled Hart, 'and they formed front in the direction I pointed to. Hardly were they in position when puffs of smoke along the ridge and the sharp crack of bullets striking the wood about us showed that the enemy had reached the ridge' (Hart-Synnot 1912: 107).

In fact, Godide's force – now swollen to about 6,000 men with the addition of local elements from the iNsukamgeni, iQwa, uDududu and iNdabakawombe *amabutho* (about 50 companies, roughly 2,500 men) – had spent the night on the ridges beyond Wombane, a little to the right of the road. They had presumably intended to ambush Pearson's column as it struggled up the pass but if so they had missed an equally golden opportunity to attack the British as they straddled the river. The men Hart had blundered into were apparently scouts from the uMxapho *ibutho*, which was resting closest to Wombane, and these had typically rushed forward once they were discovered, the sound of the firing drawing the rest of the uMxapho out behind them. In the initial confusion, however, there was little opportunity for the main body of the uMxapho to extend properly – 'We were told to advance, and, grasping our arms, we went forward packed close together like a lot of bees,' recalled a Chief Zimema 50 years later (*NM* 22 Jan 1929: 10) – and instead they streamed in a long column down the slope of Wombane on a course that would bring them out close to the point where Pearson's wagons were still crossing the river. The uMxapho were the left horn of the

Zulu advance – the centre and right elements lay beyond them, and had further to go before they swung round to crest the heights above the road.

A steep, narrow valley, full of bush at the bottom, separated the uMxapho from the spur up which the road ran, and from the British. The column had been caught by surprise, and although the men had fallen in at the sound of the first shots, the sudden appearance of the Zulu remained startling. A member of the Stanger Mounted Rifles later wrote:

> We were not long left in doubt as to where the enemy was for, looking a little further ahead, every hillside was swarming with them. Down they came, rushing on to us, and defiling as to surround us, disappearing into the bushy ravines below, soon to be seen swarming over the next ridge nearer to us, and preparing to rush down it and close with us. There seemed to be no end of them … (Quoted in Castle & Knight 1994: 59)

From Pearson's perspective it seemed that the attack was developing to the right of the road, and he hurried to bring his men up from the river to form a firing line facing it, in accordance with Chelmsford's Standing Orders. He placed his two 7-pdr guns on a low knoll just to the right of the track with a company of the Buffs under Capt Arthur Charles Jackson to their left and another under Lt Martin to their right. A company of HMS *Active*'s Naval Brigade passed up the road behind this line and formed up securing Jackson's left, looking up the track, and as other units came up from the drift they formed up below Martin, facing to their right. One man of the Buffs, L/Cpl Taylor, was so keen not to miss the action that, although sick, he left his bed in the hospital wagon to take part. Sappers of No. 2 Company, Royal Engineers had been supervising the crossing when the shooting began and their officer, Capt Warren Richard Colvin Wynne RE,

An eyewitness sketch of the height of the battle; Pearson has formed his men facing to the right of the road, while the Zulu advanced down the slopes of Wombane beyond. Note the position of the guns in the centre of the line and that the 2/3rd Regiment has its Colours unfurled; men open ammunition boxes in the foreground. (National Army Museum)

A view of the Nyezane battlefield from the summit of Wombane. The original track ran up the spur opposite, slightly above the modern road; Pearson's main position was on the knoll directly above the car (right). The uMxapho *ibutho* streamed down this hillside to the left, hoping to outflank the British column. (Author's Collection)

Determined to leave the road, and turned off to the right, and having reached a low narrow ridge, where I found the mounted infantry posted (on foot), I extended my company in skirmishing order from their (Mounted Infantry) right. We no sooner showed ourselves on the further slope of this ridge than the Zulus, who were concealed in bush 150 to 250 yards off began firing at us, bullets whizzing close by, right and left. We returned it in good earnest and I selected places of cover behind trunks of trees, etc, for my men. (Quoted in Wynne 1995: 74)

By this time, both the artillery and Jackson's and Martin's companies were fully engaged, firing at the uMxapho streaming down the slope opposite. This fire, Chief Zimema would later admit, came as something of a shock:

We were still far away from them when the white men began to throw their bullets at us, but we could not shoot them because our rifles would not shoot so far … when we were near them we opened fire, hitting a number of them … After that they brought out their [artillery and rockets] and we heard what we thought was a long pipe coming toward us. As we advanced we had our rifles under our arms and our assegais in our right hands ready to throw them but they were not much good as we never got near enough to use them. We never got nearer than 50 paces [roughly 50yd] to the English, and although we tried to climb over our fallen brothers we could not get very far ahead because the white men were firing heavily close to the ground into our front ranks whilst the [artillery] were firing over our heads into the regiments behind us … (*NM* 22 Jan 1929: 10)

Even so, the British were impressed to note that once they were clear of the exposed slopes the Zulu were able to extend and to make good use of the cover in the valley bottoms before the British line. As Col Sgt J.W. Burnett of the 99th Regiment recalled:

The men that fired did not load the guns. They would fire and run into the bush, and have fresh guns loaded for them, and out again. They fired young cannon balls, slugs, and even gravel. I tell you what it is: our 'school' at Chatham, over one hot whisky, used to laugh about these [Africans], but I assure you that fighting with them is terribly earnest work, and not child's play. Sergeant Tuckett's party, Royal Engineers, were in the thick of it, but none of the Royal Engineers were killed ... Sergeant Tuckett knocked two or three [Zulu] over ... (Quoted in Emery 1977: 185)

Lt Thomas Ryder Main RE, Commanding the First Division's half-company of No. 2 Company Natal Native Pioneers, was standing near the two guns when the officer in charge of them asked him to take temporary command of one while he moved the other. 'I found myself suddenly an active officer of RA', he recalled, and

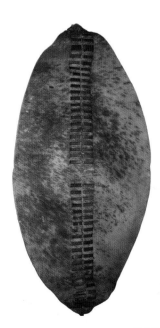

Two *izihlangu* shields of the uMxapho *ibutho*. The uMxapho were heavily engaged at Nyezane, although these particular examples were taken by the British from the royal homesteads around oNdini following the battle of Ulundi on 4 July 1879. (Author's Collection)

I must say I didn't like the look of things. Nothing seemed to stop the Zulus. They slithered through the long grass and although they suffered severely, they came nearer, and got nearer. I saw the RE sergt. who had to be left in charge of our wagons in the column came sneaking up. He had (rightly!) deserted his charge, but I took away his rifle and 24 rounds and felt happier at once. Lloyd came along and I gave him back his gun which was splattered with bullets, though with no casualties. I went down the side of the hill and there I found two old soldiers of the Buffs (officers' servants I think), one of whom, I remember, was firing away and smoking a short black pipe ... I took charge of this small party and agreed with them that we should combine in firing only at distinct figures, and then all at the same one. As the Zulus were now not 200 yards away I feel sure we did much damage, as I fired away my 24 rounds and at that range one could not well miss one's target. Some of the Zulus got to within 100 yards of our position, but could not hit home … (Quoted in Castle & Knight 1994: 63)

Although the British infantry had extended and taken use of what cover they could, they remained an easy target, even to the notoriously inaccurate Zulu marksmen. One Zulu seemed to have got the range well and, firing from the cover of a low tree, was seen to place several bullets dangerously close to their targets. A number of men fired at him in return, only for him to fall at last to a chance shot that went high – and struck him, not at the foot of the tree, but among the branches where he had been hiding.

Yet the battle was steadily turning against the Zulu. Not only, as Zimema had recognized, were they unable to penetrate the fire zone directly in front of the British lines, but the British detachments skirmishing forward from the road were beginning to drive back the point of the left horn. Moreover, the men from HMS *Active* had landed a Gatling gun – a hand-cranked rapid-fire gun – and under the command of a young midshipman, Lewis Coker, it was hurried up from the rear to the knoll and turned towards the valley below Wombane, the first time such a gun was used in action by British troops. It only managed one short burst for 30 seconds before it jammed, but the bullets chopped through the bush and immediately silenced Zulu fire from the target area.

By this time the Zulu centre and right had begun to manoeuvre to join the attack and the 'chest', largely consisting of the older uDlambedlu and izinGulube *amabutho*, began to appear at the head of the ridge directly above the road. From there they descended to occupy a deserted homestead lying just a few hundred yards up the road from Pearson's left flank. Nestling in among the huts and palisades, they opened a steady fire that enfiladed Pearson's line and, had it been better directed, might have made his position untenable. Capt Hart saw the danger, and moved to check it:

This fire coming into the backs of our troops who were engaged near the gun, I accordingly marched the company I had rallied together, with another company of natives who had been in the advanced guard, against this kraal [enclosure], but the courage of our natives utterly failed, they crouched down under any cover they could find, and after fruitless efforts to make them advance, I called upon the white men of the two companies to go with me without them. We advanced steadily against the kraal by the main road, the officers, except myself, dismounted; and the little party used their rifles well, and did as I directed, halting to fire, and advancing again when I gave the word. (Hart-Synnot 1912: 109)

At the same time, the men from HMS *Active* on Pearson's left directed a rocket into the homestead; it passed through one hut, setting it on fire. They then followed Hart's NNC men in an exuberant charge, running up the slope and firing as they went in no particular formation, much to the amusement of Army officers watching them. The Zulu centre stood its ground for a few minutes and the British advance stalled; a fire-fight developed until a further company of the Buffs, under Capt J.W. Forster, came up in support. The British renewed their advance, although two men of the Buffs were shot dead and two more wounded, one of them mortally. At last, however, the Zulu abandoned the homestead just before Hart's men reached it, and fell back up the slope. A Zulu prisoner later admitted that the Zulu thought they were winning the battle until 'those horrible men in white trousers rushed up and showered lead upon them' (quoted in Castle & Knight 1994: 67).

The Zulu right horn, too, had been checked. Advancing far too late to be of use, it had swung further round and onto yet another spur lying to the left of the road, only to run into a handful of vedettes Pearson had posted there. On coming under fire the men of the Zulu right horn assumed that the British were

The closing stages of Nyezane – while the Zulu left continues its increasingly futile attack from Wombane (right) the Zulu centre has occupied a homestead above the road. The huts are already in flames, however, fired by rockets from HMS *Active*'s Naval Brigade, and the Zulu centre will soon be driven out of the homestead altogether by an attack by NCOs of the NNC supported by the sailors. (National Army Museum)

Nyezane, 22 January 1879

Here we see the climax of the battle. In the foreground the uMxapho *ibutho*, constituting the Zulu left 'horn', streams down the slopes of Wombane Hill in an attempt to outflank the British position. Pearson's column had been advancing up the track on the opposite spur, centre, when the battle began, and his infantry and guns had deployed to their right to meet the Zulu attack. The uMxapho faced an approach down a hillside dangerously exposed to British fire before reaching the gulley that separated them from the British position. Although their attack was extremely determined, it began to stall as men took cover in the gulley from close-range British musketry.

This scene is set towards the bottom of the slope, near the extreme Zulu left; the men in the foreground are still extending to complete the turning movement, while those who have already reached the gully are engaged in a fire-fight with the British. Small groups of Zulu are attempting to charge across the short space separating them from the British lines but cannot penetrate the British curtain of fire. Realizing that the Zulu attack is losing impetus, a company of the 2/3rd Regiment opposite is beginning to advance in skirmishing order – the front rank firing and the rear rank then passing forward between the files – to clear the gully. Elsewhere, the attack of the Zulu centre – advancing directly at the head of Pearson's column – has already been checked, while the attack of the Zulu right has failed to develop; shortly after this, the uMxapho will acknowledge the futility of continuing their attack, and begin to withdraw.

Midshipman Lewis Coker of HMS *Active* directs the ship's Gatling gun at the height of the battle. Although it was in action for only a short time, this marked the first time a Gatling gun was used by British forces in battle. (Author's Collection)

equally well protected on that side and, as the Zulu main force was falling back across the battlefield, they too withdrew.

By this point the Zulu had abandoned any hope of closing with the British line and began to retire, carrying their wounded with them where they could. They were still exposed to British fire as they did so, and as they began to pass back over the skyline of Wombane. Once they had regained their breath Hart's men, with the Naval Brigade and Forster's company of the Buffs, set off in pursuit, clearing the road ahead and driving the Zulu further off beyond the summit of Wombane.

The battle was won for the British, and once the smoke cleared and the adrenaline began to wear off the victors congratulated themselves on their success – and their survival. An officer in the Natal Volunteers, Lt Robarts, confided with quiet pride to his wife that 'in action my only sensation was that of pleasurable excitement'. Nevertheless, the sight of the Zulu dead and wounded scattered across the battlefield was a sobering one, particularly for those who had not been in battle before. Robarts continued:

We then had leisure to look at the wounded men, and very pitiful it was to see the poor fellows lying with fearful wounds. They were very quiet, and seemed to bear pain well, no groaning or crying out. We could not do anything for them except give them water to drink … The vedettes found a great many dead and wounded up on the ridge – one of them had crawled at least a quarter of a mile with a broken leg. One poor fellow was in an ant bear hole about 700 yards from the vedettes in front of them, and they did not see him for a long time until he called out … It is a fearful thing to see a wounded man uncared for … The excitement is all right enough while it is on – but I do not like to think of those poor fellows left. The rockets scorch whoever they go near – we saw several bodies with burn marks on them. (Quoted in Castle & Knight 1994: 69)

This compassion was real enough in the aftermath of an early British victory – but it would not long survive the tougher fighting to come. There was little that could be done for the Zulu wounded, and they were left where they lay; British parties passing up and down the road still heard them calling out for days to come. Some, no doubt, managed to crawl away and survive, but others died days or weeks later from shock, blood loss and infection. Pearson estimated the Zulu dead at about 400 men, but given these factors it is likely they numbered into the 600s, with many more injured.

The British losses totalled 12 men killed and 20 wounded; the dead were collected up and buried in a mass grave beside the road. Pearson was keen to demonstrate that the Zulu attack had not checked him in the least and, after allowing his men a short rest, he gave the order to resume the march to Eshowe.

The Zulu, meanwhile, had retired for several miles from the battlefield in some confusion before they attempted to regroup and assess their losses. They were deeply shocked by their repulse, and in particular disappointed in the performance of their own firearms. The uMxapho, in particular, had made a determined effort to reach the British lines, but simply could not force a way through the curtain of fire, and the experience had been shocking even to those who survived. 'The battle was so fierce', recalled Chief Zimema, 'that we had to wipe the blood and brains of the killed and wounded from our heads, faces, arms, legs and shields after the fighting' (*NM* 22 Jan 1929: 10). Another warrior of the uMxapho, Sihlala, agreed:

> We fought hard but we could not beat the whites, they shot us down in numbers, in some places our dead and wounded covered the ground, we lost heavily, especially from the small guns [rifles]. Many of our men were drowned in the Nyezane river, in attempting to cross at a part of the river where it was too deep for anyone but a swimmer, in the rush made for the river several men were forced over trees and dongas [erosion gullies], and killed that way, the [rockets] killed people but the small guns are the worst. (Quoted in Castle & Knight 1994: 68)

Yet the British success masked the fact that they had been lucky at Nyezane. Pearson had been attacked while his column was on the march – a situation every British commander dreaded – but the Zulu attack had been poorly coordinated, allowing him ample time to draw up in Chelmsford's preferred formation. And, as Chelmsford had anticipated, that formation had been able to lay down sufficient firepower to check the Zulu attack. Even so, Godide had not enjoyed the degree of numerical superiority to be employed in later battles, and in fact – as the uMxapho complained bitterly afterwards – the Zulu centre and right had scarcely been deployed at all.

What might have happened had the Zulu attack been properly coordinated, and delivered in much greater strength, was to be demonstrated just a few hours later elsewhere along the Zulu border.

iSandlwana

22 January 1879

The battlefield of iSandlwana today, photographed from the old wagon-drift across the Nyogane stream. The British camp was stretched across the foot of the mountain behind; Durnford defended the stream banks against the attack of the Zulu left 'horn' (attacking from behind the camera position). This picture gives some impression of the extent of the ground covered by the British perimeter. (Author's Collection)

BACKGROUND TO BATTLE

The main Zulu army had left oNdini on 17 January, heading westwards at a leisurely pace towards Rorke's Drift. By 20 January it had reached Siphezi Mountain, no more than a day's march from the border. The poor weather had delayed Lord Chelmsford's advance at the river and it was not until 20 January that he felt able to advance to a distinctive rocky outcrop called iSandlwana. Chelmsford's own Standing Orders had specified that all permanent camps be entrenched, but in fact he did not intend to stay long at iSandlwana, and considered the camp in any case too extended to entrench properly. Rumours of the Zulu advance had already reached him, and from the moment he arrived at iSandlwana Chelmsford was focused

on the country ahead, and what it might contain. For about 12 miles beyond iSandlwana the track passed through a relatively open plain but it was shut in closer to the right by high ridges that masked broken country bordering the Mzinyathi downstream from Rorke's Drift. Chelmsford rode out with his staff to explore this country, and his main concern was that any approaching Zulu army might opt to avoid the direct approach to iSandlwana, down the open plain, and instead use the hills on his right to mask a move past his flank and into Natal. He returned to camp that evening with orders that a strong reconnaissance be made to sweep through those hills.

Accordingly, at dawn on the 21st most of the Column's mounted men and NNC set out under the overall command of a Maj John Dartnell of the Natal Mounted Police. Not until his detachments met up late that afternoon on the far side of the hills, above the spectacular Mangeni River gorge, and prepared to march back did mounted patrols spot Zulu on the crest of a hill nearby. The Zulu deployed to attack, advanced but then suddenly retired.

Dartnell decided to bivouac on the hills, and to send a message requesting Chelmsford's support. That message reached Chelmsford's tent at iSandlwana at about 0200hrs on the 22nd. The Zulu seemed to have shown their hand early, and Chelmsford had the chance to move quickly to intercept them and take them by surprise. He would take four of the Column's six guns and all but one company of the 2/24th Regiment and move out to attack the Zulu; the rest, including two guns, five companies of the 1/24th Regiment and one of the 2/24th, he would leave to guard the camp. He gave command at iSandlwana to the senior remaining officer, Lt-Col Henry Pulleine of the 1/24th Regiment, and as he was about to depart Chelmsford's staff reminded him that there were more troops available close at hand. The No. 2 Column – which consisted largely of auxiliary troops, commanded by Bvt Col Anthony Durnford RE – had originally been placed at the Middle Drift on the Thukela, but a few days earlier Chelmsford had instructed it to move instead to Rorke's Drift. Before he left the camp, Durnford sent a hasty message to Durnford ordering him forward to iSandlwana.

Yet even before Chelmsford moved to intercept them, the Zulu forces had already moved. The men Dartnell had encountered were local warriors, hurrying to join the main army, which had already shifted from its bivouac at Siphezi Mountain. Moving in small parties, so as not to attract the attention of British scouts, the *amabutho* had moved through undulating country to occupy the valley of the Ngwebeni River about 5 miles north-east of iSandlwana, and separated from the British camp by rolling uplands that blocked it from view. For a combination of religious and political reasons – and perhaps to allow the army to rest after its late march – Ntshingwayo hoped to avoid battle on the 22nd.

Chelmsford arrived at the hills along the Mangeni headwaters early in the morning and split his men into small detachments, much as he had on the Cape Frontier, and set off in pursuit. Sporadic skirmishing broke out.

The sound of that distant gunfire drifted across to the *amabutho* bivouacking in the Ngwebeni Valley. The warriors were acutely aware that the enemy lay close by, and, buoyed up by the rituals performed at oNdini, the tension among them was intense. Hearing those shots, the *amabutho* camped closest to iSandlwana – the uNokhenke and uKhandempemvu – had, without waiting for orders, left the valley and pushed across the heights in the expectation that battle had already begun. Their *izinduna* eventually managed to restore order and turn them back to the bivouac, but not before some of them had appeared on the crest of the escarpment directly above iSandlwana, and within full sight of the camp. They had only just retired from view when Durnford's command arrived at iSandlwana from along the Rorke's Drift road.

It was now about 1030hrs on 22 January. Durnford was now the senior British officer at iSandlwana but, while Pulleine was under specific orders from Chelmsford to guard the camp, Durnford found no comparable orders awaiting his arrival. It was obvious to Durnford, too, that the situation had changed since Chelmsford's departure – the Zulu movements close to the camp presented a new and unexpected threat. At about 1130hrs he sent two troops of the Sikhali (amaNgwane) Horse, under Lts Raw and Roberts, up onto the heights with orders to sweep across the top. One of his troops was still on the road, escorting his baggage, but Durnford himself set out with the remaining troops, together with a rocket battery with its NNC infantry escort, to swing round the bottom of the heights in the same direction.

INTO COMBAT

On the heights Raw and Roberts spotted small parties of Zulu foragers driving away cattle in the distance, and gave chase. Raw pursued one party who disappeared around the foot of a hill; riding up onto the shoulder to cut them off, Raw's men found themselves looking down into the Ngwebeni Valley – and the *amabutho* camped there.

In that electric moment, as the horsemen appeared suddenly on the skyline, the collective tension among the *amabutho* broke, and whatever Ntshingwayo's plans, the nearest warriors rose up and rushed to attack. 'They turned and fell upon us', reported Raw laconically, 'the whole army showing itself from behind the hill in front where they had evidently been waiting' (quoted in Knight 2010: 345). Raw dismounted his men to fire a volley, then mounted again and retired towards the camp. 'At once [they] found themselves in the close embrace of the Kandempemvu', recalled a Zulu named Muziwento, 'even as tobacco [is mixed] with aloes' (quoted in *Natalia* 8 (Dec 1978): 15).

The Zulu army spilled out of the Ngwebeni Valley in some confusion, the original order of attack forgotten. 'We sped on at the lope like a pack of wolves', a British missionary, Revd A.W. Lee, was told after the war, 'spurning the dust with our feet as we passed. Men leapt aloft like spring-bok in their eagerness to get forward to their first view of the enemy. So, running, leaping we swept up ...' (*NW* 19 Jan 1929: 18). There were, however, several miles separating them from the British camp, and their commanders, hurrying up from the rear, had time to impose some new sense of order. 'We heard firing on top of the rise', said a man named Mhlahlana of the iNgobamakosi, 'and as soon as we got on top we saw the Ukandempemvu and the white men in grips with each other. We were then brought round to get into line with the Ukandempemvu' (*NM* 22 Jan 1929: 10).

None of this was apparent to the British garrison at iSandlwana. Earlier, and probably in response to that premature Zulu movement towards the camp, Lt Walter Cavaye's E Company, 1/24th Regiment, had been sent up onto the ridges immediately north of the camp and, having passed over the skyline, had disappeared from sight. Some time later the splutter of shots from Raw's encounter could be heard, and breathless riders rode in with news of the Zulu approach. Yet Pulleine could see nothing of this from his position at the foot of the hill, and his first response was to send another company – Capt William Mostyn's F Company, 1/24th Regiment – to reinforce Cavaye. The rest of his force – two 7-pdr guns and four more companies of the 24th – Pulleine pushed forward to a position above some dongas commanding the slopes down which any Zulu attack from that direction must come. One of the column's transport officers, Maj Edward Essex, noted some telling facts about the Zulu opposite them:

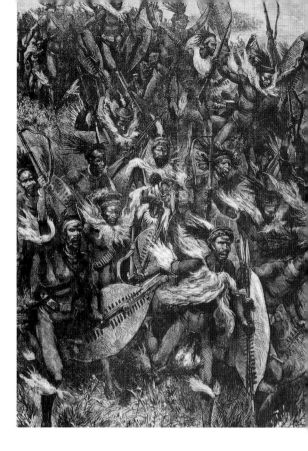

A Zulu attack. Although the artist has generally captured the appearance of the warriors well – including the number of firearms – in fact the Zulu approached in a more extended order, and only concentrated like this for a final rush, such as occurred at iSandlwana. (Author's Collection)

> The Zulus returned our fire but it was very wild, and nearly every shot fell short or went over our heads. Their line was about 1000 yards in extent, but arranged like a horn, that is, very thin and extended on their right but gradually thickening towards ours. They did not advance but moved steadily towards our left, each man running from rock to rock, for the ground here was covered with large boulders, with the evident intent of outflanking us. The company 1st bttn, 24th which I had passed en route took up its position on our left on its arrival and entered into action as did a body of natives on our right. I did not notice the latter much save that they blazed away at an absurd rate. The movement of the Zulus towards our left still continued, and their line, which was now assuming a circular form, appeared to be constantly fed from their left, and was constantly increasing and thickening in that direction. They skirmished very beautifully, and I saw that very few, considering we now had about 3000 opposed to us, were hit. (*Times* 12 Apr 1879)

It was, perhaps, as good a description of a deploying 'horn' as was ever written by someone who witnessed it.

MAP KEY

1 Night of 22/23 January: The Zulu army masses along the banks of the Ngwebeni River, behind Mabaso Hill.

2 Early morning, 22 January: Elements of the uNokhenke and uKhandempemvu *amabutho* press forward to the edge of the iNyoni Ridge. They are then withdrawn to the bivouac.

3 1030hrs (approx.): Capt Cavaye's E Company, 1/24th Regiment, is sent onto the ridge in response. Cavaye detaches a section under 2/Lt Dyson to protect his left flank.

4 1030hrs: Col Durnford arrives at iSandlwana.

5 1130hrs: Durnford despatches Lt Raw's No. 1 Troop and Lt Roberts' No. 2 Troop of the Sikhali Horse across the heights.

6 1145hrs (approx.): Durnford, Lt Davies' Edendale Troop and Lt Henderson's Hlubi (Tlokoa) Troop leave the camp.

7 1200hrs (approx.): Raw pursues Zulu foragers around Mabaso Hill; the uKhandempemvu rush forward to attack Raw's men, drawing the entire Zulu army out of the valley.

8 1215hrs (approx.): Durnford encounters the Zulu left 'horn' – the uVe *ibutho* – and begins a fighting withdrawal.

9 1230hrs (approx.): Cavaye is reinforced by Capt Mostyn's F Company, 1/24th Regiment.

10 1230hrs (approx.): The Zulu army deploys on the high ground, much of it still out of sight from Durnford and Pulleine.

11 1230hrs (approx.): Pulleine deploys Maj S. Smith RA's two 7-pdr guns on a rise, supported by Capt Wardell's H Company and Lt Porteous' A Company, 1/24th Regiment; Lt Pope's G Company, 2/24th Regiment, and Capt J.F. Lonsdale's No. 9 Company, 1/3rd NNC form the right of this line.

12 1240hrs (approx.): Maj Russell RA's three 9-pdr rocket troughs lag behind Durnford and become isolated; they deploy, but are overrun by the skirmishers of the iNgobamakhosi.

13 1250hrs (approx.): Finding the Nyogane stream defended by a detachment of Natal Volunteers, Durnford deploys his own men beside them, in order to hold back the Zulu left 'horn'.

14 1300hrs (approx.): After engaging the Zulu right 'horn', Cavaye and Mostyn's companies withdraw to the foot of the ridge and join the line already established there.

15 1310hrs (approx.): The uVe and the iNgobamakhosi extend to the left, threatening to outflank Durnford downstream.

16 1310hrs (approx.): Elements of the uMbonambi occupy the Nyogane upstream from Durnford, and begin to probe the gap between Durnford and Pulleine's line.

17 1310hrs (approx.): Entering the valley behind iSandlwana, the Zulu right 'horn' cuts the road to Rorke's Drift.

18 1315hrs (approx.): Durnford's position becomes untenable and he abandons the Nyogane and retires towards the camp.

19 1325hrs (approx.): Durnford's withdrawal is followed by Pulleine's. The uKhandempemvu launch a fresh assault, spurring a renewed attack; the British position soon collapses.

20 1345hrs (approx.): The uNokhenke *ibutho* shifts its line of attack to its right and passes behind iSandlwana, entering the camp from the Rorke's Drift road.

21 1345–1430hrs (approx.): The British infantry companies withdraw through the camp under heavy Zulu attack; the last surviving groups are forced off the road by the right 'horn'.

22 1430–1500hrs (approx.): The last organized British resistance takes place on the banks of the Manzimnyama. The Zulu right and left 'horns' do not quite meet, however, allowing a number of British survivors to escape through the gap.

23 1430–1530hrs (approx.): The Zulu reserve (the uThulwana, iNdlondlo, iNdluyengwe and uDloko), with the right 'horn', harry British survivors as far as the Mzinyathi before entering Natal.

Battlefield environment

An established traders' track crossed into Zululand by way of an established ford, known as Rorke's Drift. Once across the Mzinyathi, Lord Chelmsford would be advancing with undulating country to his front and left, but with broken, rugged, mountainous terrain on his right. With the coming of the summer rains, the grass here, too, was tall – waist-high or more – green, and often wet. At times, on the eve of the invasion, the rain was so severe as to wash away tents in the British camp; although the landscape dried out again in the heat of the day the soil remained damp. Beyond Rorke's Drift, the track passed below the southern edge of a rocky outcrop known as iSandlwana before crossing some ten miles of relatively open plain, framed by ridges on either side, and again disappearing into the far hills. For Chelmsford, iSandlwana was perhaps not an ideal camp site, but it offered water, firewood and forage for his men and animals, a commanding view to his front, and the hill itself to protect his rear.

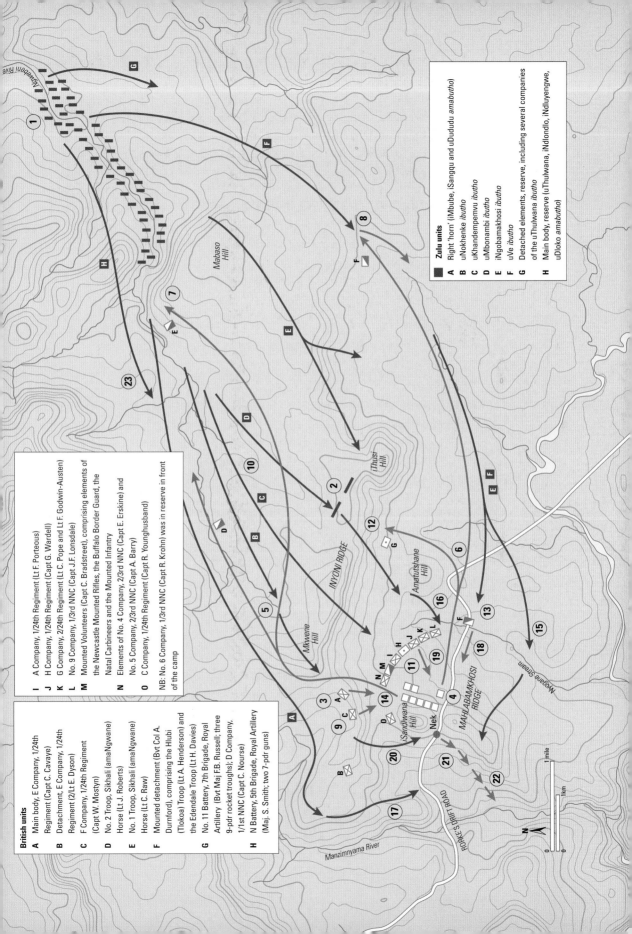

British units

A Main body, E Company, 1/24th Regiment (Capt C. Cavaye)
B H Company, 1/24th Regiment (Capt G. Wardell)
C Detachment, E Company, 1/24th Regiment (2/Lt E. Dyson)
D F Company, 1/24th Regiment (Capt W. Mostyn)
E No. 2 Troop, Sikhali (amaNgwane) Horse (Lt J. Roberts)
F No. 1 Troop, Sikhali (amaNgwane) Horse (Lt C. Raw)
G Mounted detachment (Bvt Col A. Durnford), comprising the Hlubi (Tlokoa) Troop (Lt A. Henderson) and the Edendale Troop (Lt H. Davies)
H No. 11 Battery, 7th Brigade, Royal Artillery (Bvt Maj F.B. Russell; three 9-pdr rocket troughs); D Company, 1/1st NNC (Capt C. Nourse)
N N Battery, 5th Brigade, Royal Artillery (Maj. S. Smith; two 7-pdr guns)

I A Company, 1/24th Regiment (Lt F. Porteous)
J H Company, 1/24th Regiment (Capt C. Cavaye)
K G Company, 2/24th Regiment (Lt C. Pope and Lt F. Godwin-Austen)
L No. 9 Company, 1/3rd NNC (Capt J.F. Lonsdale)
M Mounted Volunteers (Capt C. Bradstreet), comprising elements of the Newcastle Mounted Rifles, the Buffalo Border Guard, the Natal Carbineers and the Mounted Infantry
N Elements of No. 4 Company, 2/3rd NNC (Capt E. Erskine) and No. 5 Company, 2/3rd NNC (Capt A. Barry)
O C Company, 1/24th Regiment (Capt R. Younghusband)

NB: No. 6 Company, 1/3rd NNC (Capt R. Krohn) was in reserve in front of the camp

Zulu units

A Right 'horn' (iMbube, iSangqu and uDududu *amabutho*)
B uNokhenke *ibutho*
C uKhandempemvu *ibutho*
D uMbonambi *ibutho*
E iNgobamakhosi *ibutho*
F uVe *ibutho*
G Detached elements, reserve, including several companies of the uThulwana *ibutho*
H Main body, reserve (uThulwana, iNdlondlo, iNdluyengwe, uDloko *amabutho*)

By this point the Zulu attack was fully developed. The right 'horn', the men observed by Essex, were the iSangqu, uDududu and iMbube *amabutho*. Next to them, and now extended in long lines screened by skirmishers, were the uNokhehke, uKhandempemvu and uMbonambi, while further off was the left 'horn' – the iNgobamakhosi and, separated by the ground, the young men of the uVe. Mixed in with these were a few companies from other *amabutho* who were fighting elsewhere but who had arrived too late for the general muster, and had joined this army on the march. Ntshingwayo had managed to hold back only a few senior *amabutho* associated with the king's royal homestead at oNdini – the uThulwana, iNdlondlo, uDloko and iNdluyengwe – and these had been formed into a reserve, and set to follow behind the right 'horn' with the intention of cutting the road to Rorke's Drift.

Much of this attack was hidden from the British until the first skirmishers from the 'chest' began to descend the escarpment. Their appearance threatened to cut off the various British detachments already engaged on the heights and Pulleine sent a hurried order to recall his men, and Mostyn and Cavaye's companies fell back, mixed up with Raw and Roberts' men.

Durnford himself, meanwhile, had ridden 4 or 5 miles and was lost to sight from the camp. His rocket battery – three 9-pdr rocket troughs carried on mules and commanded by Bvt Maj Francis Russell RA and escorted by D Company, 1/1st NNC under Capt Nourse – had lagged considerably behind and become separated. Durnford, too, had noticed small parties of foragers to his front and was about to pursue them when the young uVe *ibutho*, the tip of the left 'horn', suddenly appeared over a rise in front of him. It was obvious that Durnford was heavily outnumbered and he ordered his men to make a fighting withdrawal towards the camp. By this time Russell's command was completely isolated and had begun to climb the escarpment towards the unfolding Zulu attack. The crews had only just managed to set up the troughs when the skirmishers of the iNgobamakhosi swept down and overran them. The Zulu did not press their success, of course, because they knew that the main body of the iNgobamakhosi would be up soon enough, and Nourse managed to rally a handful of his men to trade shots with the Zulu among boulders at the foot of the slope.

In the mean time, the main body of the 'chest', the uNokhenke, uKhandempemvu and uMbonambi, had begun to spill over the skyline along the length of the ridge. The uNokhenke were caught briefly against the crest by the fire of Mostyn and Cavaye's companies, and retired to regroup before shifting to their right. The uKhandempemvu and uMbonambi swept on in fine style, however, and were now in full view of the British positions, as Lt Horace Smith-Dorrien of the 95th Regiment, a junior transport officer, recalled: '[They] showed in large numbers, coming down into the plain with great boldness … It was a marvellous sight, line upon line of men in slightly extended order, one behind the other, firing as they came along' (Smith-Dorrien 1925: 13).

As the Zulu centre pushed down the escarpment towards Pulleine's line, the two 7-pdr guns opened fire with shrapnel shells. The British had by now fallen into a rough line facing north. In the centre were the guns, supported to the left by Lt F. Porteous' A Company, 1/24th Regiment, and to the right by Capt G. Wardell's H Company, 1/24th Regiment. Mostyn and Cavaye's companies were to the left of Porteous, and the detachments of NNC and Raw and Roberts' troops were next to them, while the far left was anchored by Capt R. Younghusband's C Company, 1/24th Regiment. To the right of Wardell was G Company, 2/24th Regiment – left in the camp that morning to provide picquets when the rest of the battalion marched out with Chelmsford – under Lt C. Pope and Lt F. Godwin-Austen, and next to them Capt James Lonsdale's No. 9 Company, 1/3rd NNC. Beyond that, there was nothing – until Durnford re-appeared, with the Zulu left in hot pursuit.

Durnford had continued his fighting withdrawal until he reached the bed of a stream, the Nyogane, which flows across the plain about a mile from iSandlwana. Here he dismounted his men and took up positions nestling into the bank facing the Zulu. Upstream from Durnford, the *dongas* forming the Nyogane curved leisurely eastwards, draining the hollows at the foot of the high ground. Descending the escarpment, the Zulu centre had occupied these *dongas*, which offered them some shelter from the British fire, but once in them had found it difficult to get out. Ahead of them the ground rose slightly for 300–400yd towards the 24th Regiment's line – and any attack would have to be made up that slope, exposed to the full weight of the fire from the 24th Regiment's companies.

The men of the 24th Regiment were using the ground well, although their line was stretched very thinly; the companies were again in extended order, the men kneeling or lying down, and the intervals between them probably greater than the distances specified by the manuals. The Zulu attack seemed to have stalled in front of them, and the men were in good spirits. Essex noted that 'the 24th men ... were as cheery as possible, making remarks to one another about their shooting, and the enemy opposed to them made little progress' (*Times* 12 Apr 1879). Their fire was certainly impressive and further

Once the rifle companies of the 24th Regiment abandoned their forward position and retired towards the tents the Zulu skill at close-quarter combat, combined with their superior numbers, began to tell, and the British infantry companies were steadily broken down into small knots and overwhelmed. (Author's Collection)

back in the camp, the civilian Brickhill was convinced it was costing the Zulu dear: 'I could see nothing of the infantry fighting because of the low-laying land but, if the unceasing firing they kept up was any indication at all, then the enemy's losses must have been terrible indeed' (*Natal* Sep 1879: 257).

In the ranks of the uKhandempemvu, a warrior named uMhoti confirmed that 'when the soldiers who lay on the flat in front of the camp poured volley after volley into the *impi* we crouched down and dared not advance a step'; he noted, however, that some may not have adjusted their sights correctly since 'the soldiers fired low, most of the bullets striking the ground in front of us, and ricocheting over the foremost men' (quoted in Symons n.d.: 76). Even so, the experience of being on the receiving end of that fire was arguably even more intense than that Chief Zimema had described at Nyezane.

At this point the battle seemed destined to repeat the pattern of Nyezane, earlier that day. Yet there were important differences. The musketry of the 24th Regiment may have stalled the 'chest', but any impression of imminent British victory missed the point that the Zulu commanded a much greater sweep of ground than at Nyezane, that all the *amabutho* at iSandlwana were committed to the attack, and that as a result the Zulu enjoyed a greater numerical superiority than they had at Nyezane. Given the distance between the Zulu 'horns' – and the fact that the Zulu right had largely disappeared from view since it had passed before Mostyn and Cavaye's companies at the start of the battle – the British line was spread dangerously thinly.

Just how thin became apparent when, aware he was being outflanked, Durnford was forced to abandon the Nyogane. It was a move that effectively left the right of Pulleine's line hanging in the air. There was nothing but distance now to prevent the left horn completely outflanking the British position. The companies of the 24th Regiment retired slowly, the men falling back on the centre to form 'receive cavalry' squares. Moreover, as the guns also limbered up to withdraw and the NNC moved quickly towards the rear, large gaps began to appear in the British line.

Even before the British withdrawal, the Zulu generals, watching the battle from an excellent vantage point on the escarpment behind the 'chest', had realized that the crisis of the battle was at hand. Seeing the uKhandempemvu stalled, Ntshingwayo had despatched one of his staff, Mkhosana kaMvundlana, down to urge them on. Mkhosana strode among them, calling out in the name of the king for them to rise up and charge. Stung by this appeal to their honour, 'they all shouted "Usuthu!", and waving their shields charged the soldiers with great fury' (quoted in Mitford 1883: 27). As they did so, Mkhosana himself fell with a bullet through his head, but the moment was a decisive one, and all along the line the Zulu pressed forward.

Behind the British camp, watching from the slopes of iSandlwana Hill, the interpreter Brickhill noted ominously that 'a simultaneous forward movement was now made by all the Zulus' (quoted in *NM Supp* 1879: 258). Maj Essex noted the speed at which the British line suddenly crumpled:

> I noticed a number of native infantry retreating in haste towards the camp, their officers endeavouring to prevent them, but without effect. On looking round to that portion of the field to our right and rear I saw that the enemy was surrounding us. I rode up to Lt.Col. Durnford, who was near the right, and pointed this out to him. He requested me to take men to that part of the field and endeavour to hold the enemy in check; but while he was speaking, those men of the Native Contingent who had remained in action rushed past us in the utmost disorder, thus laying open the right and rear of the companies of the 1st Battalion 24th Regiment on the left, and the enemy dashing forward in the most rapid manner poured in at this part of the line … (Quoted in Knight 2010: 397)

In that final rush, the even spacing that had characterized the Zulu advance gave way under pressure of their contracting front, concentrating their strength for the final assault. Many Zulu took the opportunity to fire one last round from their firearms before putting them aside or leaving them on the ground.

Just before they reached the enemy there was time, too, to fling their throwing spears. Yet the infantry companies still remained dangerous. They retired slowly in the best order they could manage, firing at the Zulu as they went and keeping them from closing hand-to-hand. Even at this stage the survivors of the 24th Regiment probably still hoped to rally behind the camp. But the Zulu attack was too intense, and the standing tents hampered them, and they fought on instead as individual companies. When they reached the saddle of land below iSandlwana – the so-called nek – a fresh Zulu movement destroyed any hope of further retreat by way of the road. The movements of the Zulu right had gone largely unnoticed since the beginning of the battle but, according to an unnamed warrior of the uNokhenke,

While the Kandempemvu were driving back the horsemen over the hill north of the camp, we worked round behind Isandhlwana under cover of the long grass and dongas, intending to join the Ngobamakosi on the 'neck', and sweep in upon the camp. Then we saw the white men beginning to run away along the road to [Rorke's Drift]; many of these were cut off and killed … Our regiment went over into the camp. The ground is high and full of dongas and stones, and the soldiers did not see us until we were right upon them … (Quoted in Mitford 1883: 94)

A warrior named uMhoti, who had pushed through the British centre in the ranks of the uKhandempemvu, described how the 24th Regiment's remaining formations were steadily broken up:

One party of soldiers came out from among the tents and formed up a little above the ammunition wagons. They held their ground there until their ammunition failed them, when they were nearly all assegaid. Those that were not killed in this place formed up again in a solid square in the neck of Sandhlwana [*sic*]. They were completely surrounded on all sides, and stood back to back, and surrounding some men who were in the centre. Their ammunition was now done, except that they had some revolvers which they fired at us at close quarters. We were quite unable to break up their square until we had killed a great many of them, by throwing our assegais at short distances. We eventually overcame them in this way. (Quoted in Symons n.d.: 76).

Mehlokazulu kaSihayo noted that the long reach of the Martini-Henry and 'lunger' bayonet still made the rifle a formidable weapon, even when fighting an enemy equipped for close-quarter combat:

Some Zulus threw assegais at them, others shot at them; but they did not get close – they avoided the bayonet; for any man who went up to stab a soldier was fixed through the throat or stomach, and at once fell. Occasionally when a soldier was engaged with a Zulu in front with an assegai, another Zulu killed him from behind. (Quoted in *NM Supp* 1879: 350)

A warrior named uGuku of the uKhandempemvu

… attacked a soldier whose bayonet pierced my shield and while he was trying to extract it I stabbed him in the shoulder. He dropped his rifle and seized me round the neck and threw me on the ground under him, my eyes felt as if they were bursting and I almost choked when I succeeded in grasping the spear which was still sticking in his shoulder and forced it into his vitals and he rolled over, lifeless. (Quoted in Colenso & Durnford 1880: 413)

Mlamula Matebula of the iNgobamakhosi, who had been hit three times during the rush, was wounded again during a fight with one of the African auxiliaries fighting alongside the British:

I approached him, he struck first with the spear, I lifted my shield to guard, but unfortunately too high and it caught me on my forearm. I jumped upon him, banged him with my shield on his face and speared him. He fell down dead and I praised myself in the name of my regiment. There was a soldier who had alone killed very many of our men. There were heaps of dead bodies in front of him, he was taking shelter behind two aloe trees which were growing together, when spears were thrown at him he dodged behind one of these aloe trees. We were a lot of us attacking this man [but] when they saw others dropped down by the firing of this soldier they hesitated, and the onward rush checked. I pushed them aside, flew at him and stabbed him at close-quarters, praising myself, and killed him. He was wearing a red jacket and a cap with a tuft of wool on it. (Quoted in *Ilanga* 20 Jun 1936: 9)

In this, the last stage of the battle, the restrained tension that had prevailed among the *amabutho* since they had undergone the preparatory rituals at oNdini was released in a rush of adrenaline. Many warriors afterwards described themselves as being consumed by an excited emotional state they characterized as 'seeing nothing but red'. 'During the first phase of the battle', admitted Nzuzi Mandla, 'our eyes were dark and we stabbed everything we came across' (quoted in *NM* 22 Jan 1879: 10). Far from the heroic imagery of 'last stands' beloved by Victorian illustrators, the very end of the battle was marked by an almost medieval level of brutal slaughter:

The grim reality of death in Zululand is starkly conveyed in this eyewitness sketch of the first British burial expedition to iSandlwana on 21 May 1879. When this picture appeared as an engraving in the British press it was discreetly censored, and the macabre representation of dead soldiers in the centre replaced instead by long grass. (Author's Collection)

Some seized their rifles and smashing them down upon the rocks hurled them. They helped one another too; they stabbed those with the bayonet who sought to kill their comrades. Some covered their faces with their hands, not wishing to see death. Some ran away. Some entered into tents. Others were indignant; although badly wounded, they died where they stood, at their posts. (Quoted in *Natalia* 8 (Dec 1978): 16)

Not one officer or man who fought in the front-line companies of the 24th Regiment survived the battle. Durnford was killed, and so too was Pulleine, and the two 7-pdr guns were overtaken and over-run as they tried to flee the camp. Yet Durnford's stand in the Nyogane, and the stout defence of the companies on the nek, had served a purpose, for the two Zulu 'horns' never did quite meet behind iSandlwana, and through the shifting gap between them some men on the British side did escape. Yet of the 1,700 men in the camp when the battle began, over 1,300 had been killed, and of the survivors the vast majority were auxiliaries who had been quick enough to run one step ahead of the pursuing Zulu.

At least 1,000 Zulu had been killed outright in the attack on the camp, and perhaps an equal number mortally wounded. Hundreds – perhaps thousands – more bore terrible injuries from Martini-Henry rifle bullets, stab wounds from bayonets or sword-cuts. There was no organized system of casualty evacuation in the Zulu army, and it was left to friends and relatives to tend to them as best they could.

That evening, when Lord Chelmsford and his command finally returned to iSandlwana, they found the camp devastated and littered with the dead. Apart from a few stragglers, drunk on spirits they found in the tents, the great Zulu army had disappeared, returned to the bivouac on the Ngwebeni carrying away its wounded and its loot. Far off, down the road to Natal, the hills around the supply depot at Rorke's Drift, where Lord Chelmsford had started his invasion just 11 days before, were lit up with fire.

Khambula

29 March 1879

BACKGROUND TO BATTLE

In the aftermath of iSandlwana, the Zulu reserve – the senior men of the uThulwana, iNdlondlo, uDloko and iNdluyengwe *amabutho* – decided, despite King Cetshwayo's orders to the contrary, to cross into Natal. Of these perhaps 3,500 men went on to attack Rorke's Drift. Warned by survivors from iSandlwana of their approach, the garrison – scarcely 150 men altogether –

The attack on the hospital building at Rorke's Drift. The Zulu have carried the barricades in front of the veranda and are trying to force their way into the building itself. Although they were successful in overwhelming this part of the defences, their vulnerability in the face of concentrated British firepower directed from behind fortifications led to their failure in the battle as a whole, and paved the way for future British tactical successes. (Author's Collection)

opted to barricade the post with a stockpile of supplies that had been due to go forward to the camp at iSandlwana that day, and after ten hours of fighting that sputtered through the night the Zulu were driven off.

The battle of Rorke's Drift was not important strategically – it did not alter the fact that No. 3 (Centre) Column had largely ceased to exist as an operational unit – but it offered the British a crucial boost in morale. And it offered important tactical lessons too: Rorke's Drift had demonstrated that even a small number of men with rifles, kept together in tight formations and protected by barricades, could successfully withstand attacks by forces greatly outnumbering them.

This realization had an immediate effect on the remaining British columns operating in Zululand. Upon hearing from Chelmsford about the disaster, Pearson decided to entrench the position at Eshowe and remain where he was. In northern Zululand, however, Evelyn Wood had left his own forward base and was actually engaged in skirmishing across the foot of Hlobane Mountain when a messenger brought news of iSandlwana. 'When Col. Wood heard this', remarked Cpl Guthrie of the 90th Light Infantry somewhat wryly, 'he thought of his own small camp, 3 days in rear of him. He ordered a return march at once and marched night and day until he got to camp' (quoted in Macdougall 1998: 57).

On 31 January Wood shifted his camp several miles to a more defensible position known as Khambula, chosen for a natural combination of open views, a clear field of fire with, at the centre, a low, narrow ridge that could serve as a defensive feature. On a high point in the centre of the ridge Wood ordered the digging of a slim earthwork. On the open slope below and to the west of this fort his wagons were drawn up in a laager, or protective circle; this, too, was entrenched. A smaller entrenched laager, used to shelter the oxen, was built on the south side; a wooden palisade connected it to the fort. To the north of the camp the ground dropped away across a mostly open grassy slope. To the south, however, the ground descended in a series of terraces into a deeper valley. On this side, while Wood's positions completely commanded the immediate approach to the laagers, the valley itself was dead ground, sheltered from British fire.

From Khambula Wood raided local settlements, destroying huts and rounding up cattle throughout February and March 1879. During this time Cetshwayo had allowed his *amabutho* to rest and recuperate. By the middle of March Chelmsford, reinforced from the UK, was ready to return to the offensive; his first objective was to relieve Pearson,

A senior Zulu man of the age of the uThulwana *ibutho* and wearing the ceremonial costume associated with them – a headband of otter-skin below his head-ring, bunches of feathers from the isakabuli finch on either side of his head, and a single long crane feather (curving back here) at the front. The uThulwana and its associated *amabutho* took part in the attack on the mission station at Rorke's Drift in the aftermath of iSandlwana. (Author's Collection)

surrounded at Eshowe, and in order to confuse the Zulu as to his intention he had instructed his remaining commanders to mount diversionary attacks where they could. When Cetshwayo again ordered his *amabutho* to assemble at oNdini they came in good spirits. It was felt that Wood's persistent harrying of Zulu loyalists in the northern sector posed the greater danger. Ntshingwayo, the victor of iSandlwana, was appointed to field command again, the Zulu force being accompanied by the army's commander-in-chief, Mnyamana Buthelezi. On 24 March the army set off northwards to confront Wood, and in his final address to his warriors the king stressed the lesson of Rorke's Drift, urging them not to attack entrenched positions. 'Do not put your face into the lair of the wild beasts', he said pointedly, 'for you are sure to get clawed'.

Wood decided to resume his attack on Hlobane and on 27 March despatched his mounted troops to attack the mountain at either end at dawn the following morning, but the British were driven off Hlobane with heavy casualties. That night, the main Zulu army bivouacked between Hlobane and Khambula. The Hlobane disaster gave the British ample warning of the Zulu intentions, and Wood was determined to meet them on his own terms. Early on the 29th, the iNgobamakhosi and uVe swung out in a great arc to form the right 'horn' passing into the open country north of the camp, while the left horn – the uKhandempemvu, uMbonambi and uNokhenke – passed into the valley south of the camp and out of sight. The earlier rivalry between the iNgobamakhosi and uKhandempemvu had been exacerbated by a further dispute over the honours at iSandlwana, and the two horns pressed considerably ahead of the chest – the iNdluyengwe, iNdlondlo, uThulwana, uDloko, uDududu, iSangqu and iMbube *amabutho* – who advanced more slowly along the higher ground between the horns.

The British could see them approach across miles of countryside, and at about 1300hrs Wood ordered the alarm sounded. There would be none of the extended formations that had proved so disastrous at iSandlwana; instead, the men in the laagers knelt in the wagon beds, shoulder to shoulder, or lay underneath them, resting their rifles on the sod wall. Wood had placed a company of the 90th Light Infantry and 150 men of the 1/13th Light Infantry in the earthwork redoubt, with two field guns, while two more companies of

A sketch by Chelmsford's principal staff officer, Lt-Col John Crealock, of Wood's position at Khambula. The redoubt dominates the rise, centre, with the main laager in front of it and the cattle-laager to the right. The Zulu approached the position from beyond the hills to the right of the picture; the left 'horn' advanced up the valley on the right while the right 'horn' swung round to the more open ground on the left here. (Sherwood Foresters Museum, Nottingham)

MAP KEY

1 1330hrs (approx.): The Zulu right 'horn' – the uVe and iNgobamakhosi *amabutho* – arrives prematurely on the battlefield and begins to deploy for attack.

2 1340hrs (approx.): A foray by mounted troops under Bvt Lt-Col R. Buller provokes the right 'horn'; the mounted troops withdraw to the laager with the Zulu in pursuit.

3 1345hrs (approx.): The attack of the Zulu right 'horn' is met by musketry and artillery fire from along the north face of the British positions.

4 1400hrs (approx.): The Zulu left 'horn' advances up the valley south of the ridge, out of sight of the British, but its progress is hampered by boggy ground along the stream banks.

5 1440hrs (approx.): Elements of the uKhandempemvu occupy the camp's dung-heaps and open a heavy fire on the cattle-laager, forcing Wood to withdraw some of the men of the 1/13th Light Infantry stationed there.

6 1445hrs (approx.): The Zulu right 'horn' fails to penetrate the British defences. After holding its ground for some time it is compelled to retire to the shelter of some rocks, protected from British fire, to regroup.

7 1450hrs (approx.): Making good use of the dead ground, and supported by fire from the uKhandempemvu, the uNokhenke succeed in capturing the cattle-laager.

8 1500hrs (approx.): The British artillery is repositioned; two guns attempt to shell the Zulu right in its new sheltered position, while two more direct their fire at the uNokhenke in the cattle-laager.

9 1500hrs (approx.): The Zulu 'chest' – the iMbube, uDududu, iSangqu, uThulwana, iNdlondlo, iNdluyengwe and uDloko *amabutho* – begins a series of assaults against the eastern end of the British positions. Although some of the Zulu dead fall against the foot of the redoubt, they cannot penetrate the cordon of British fire.

10 1500hrs (approx.): With both flanks protected, the uKhandempemvu and uMbonambi mass in the valley and prepare to charge the British positions.

11 1510hrs (approx.): Two companies of the 90th Light Infantry under Maj R. Hackett sortie from the main laager and line the head of the valley, firing down into the uKhandempemvu and uMbonambi massing below. Hackett's fire disrupts the Zulu concentrations, but his men suffer from a heavy flanking fire from the dung-heaps and cattle-laager. Hackett himself is seriously wounded and his men are forced to retire.

12 1630–1730hrs (approx.): The Zulu right 'horn' makes a further assault, this time towards the redoubt, but is again repulsed by the defenders. Piecemeal Zulu attacks continue on all sides for some time, although they are increasingly uncoordinated and the warriors becoming exhausted. Finally, some *amabutho* begin an orderly withdrawal and Wood sends his mounted troops to drive them from the field. Order collapses among the Zulu and they suffer heavy casualties during the retreat.

Battlefield environment

The countryside in which Wood's command operated was very different from the sub-tropical theatre crossed by Pearson's column at the coast. Much further inland, and lying closer to the mountains, the country was largely open, broken here and there by chains of flat-topped hills and isolated stony kopjes. The rivers that were such commanding features of the central and eastern parts of the country had exerted less influence on the landscape here, and most flowed lazily through shallow beds and broad valleys. The country was thinly populated on both sides of the border, although a powerful group of Zulu royalists, the abaQulusi, lived in the countryside beyond the Hlobane and Zungwini mountains, some 15 miles to the north-east. An old Boer hunters' track wound through the border regions hugging the mountain foothills, but there were few enough established routes into Zululand, and for the most part Wood would have to march across country, making his own roads as he went. Here and there bush grew in the valleys or on the boulder-strewn hill-sides but for the most part the vista was one of unending grassland. At times the wind blew keenly across the heights and mist and drizzle sometimes settled upon them for days on end; at others, when the sun shone brightly, there were uninterrupted views across miles of country.

Wood's first base on Zululand, Fort Thinta, was built at the foot of a pointed kopje and screened by a shallow river meandering around the base but it offered few tactical strengths in the event of a concentrated attack, and in the aftermath of iSandlwana Wood moved north to Khambula. Lying on top of an open, breezy ridge, this was situated squarely across the Zulu approach towards the Boer frontier settlement at Utrecht and afforded much greater command of the ground. From the elevated summit Wood could see miles into Zululand, and the eastern and northern approaches were largely devoid of cover and fully exposed to his firepower. Only on the southern side, where the ground dipped steeply down scarcely a hundred yards from the British camp, could an approaching Zulu army hope to find any shelter.

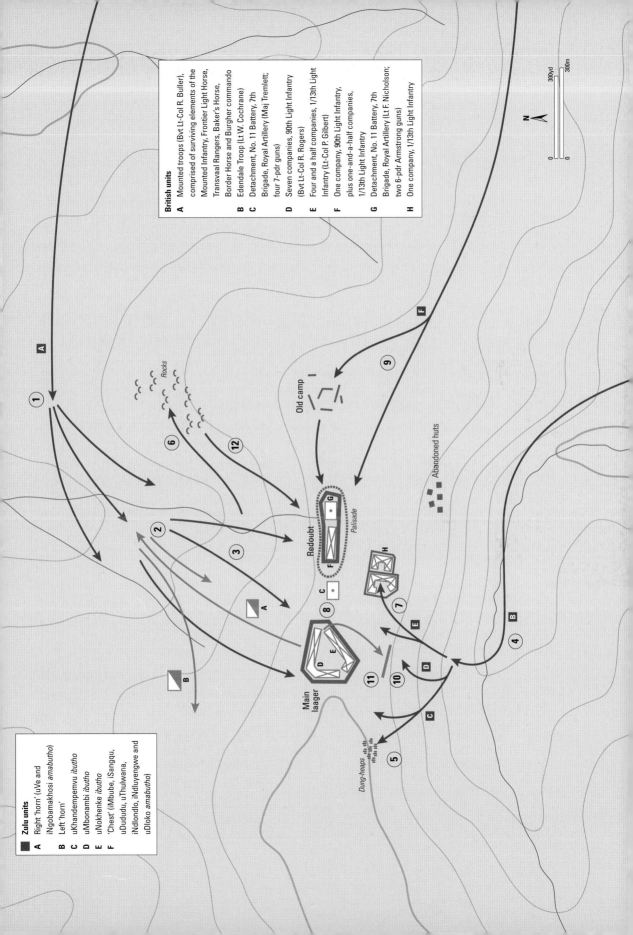

Zulu units

A Right 'horn' (uVe and iNgobamakhosi *amabutho*)
B Left 'horn'
C uKhandempemvu *ibutho*
D uMbonambi *ibutho*
E uNokhenke *ibutho*
F 'Chest' (iMbube, iSangqu, uDududu, uThulwana, iNdlondlo, iNdluyengwe and uDloko *amabutho*)

British units

A Mounted troops (Bvt Lt-Col R. Buller), comprised of surviving elements of the Mounted Infantry, Frontier Light Horse, Transvaal Rangers, Baker's Horse, Border Horse and Burgher commando
B Edendale Troop (Lt W. Cochrane)
C Detachment, No. 11 Battery, 7th Brigade, Royal Artillery (Maj Tremlett; four 7-pdr guns)
D Seven companies, 90th Light Infantry (Bvt Lt-Col R. Rogers)
E Four and a half companies, 1/13th Light Infantry (Lt-Col P. Gilbert)
F One company, 90th Light Infantry, plus one-and-a-half companies, 1/13th Light Infantry
G Detachment, No. 11 Battery, 7th Brigade, Royal Artillery (Lt F. Nicholson; two 6-pdr Armstrong guns)
H One company, 1/13th Light Infantry

Rocks

Old camp

Abandoned huts

Palisade

Redoubt

Main laager

Dung-heaps

N

300yd
300m

the 1/13th Light Infantry were guarding the cattle-laager (where some 2,000 head of cattle were still corralled). The remaining companies of the 1/13th Light Infantry held the southern side of the main laager, and the 90th Light Infantry the northern. The remaining four guns unlimbered in the open between the main laager and the redoubt.

INTO COMBAT

When the Zulu force was about 1½ miles away from the camp the right horn halted and began to deploy for action, fanning out from a column into lines and sending ahead skirmishers who rushed rapidly forward before halting again about a mile from the camp. The other *amabutho* had disappeared into the landscape, and it seems the advance of the right 'horn' was premature, although it is not clear whether by design – to beat their rivals the uKhandempemvu into the camp – or through the mistaken belief that the rest of the army was also in place.

For Wood, it was a golden opportunity; watching the army approach he had been seriously concerned that a well-coordinated attack on all sides at once might be too strong for him, and he spotted an opportunity to provoke the Zulu into launching their attacks piecemeal. He ordered his mounted troops to ride out close to the iNgobamakhosi and uVe, and to try to sting them into attacking. George Mossop, a 16-year-old trooper in the Frontier Light Horse, left a graphic account of what happened next: 'As we drew nearer to the enemy the mass became larger and larger, and when at length we dismounted and fired a volley into them, it appeared to me like a mosquito stinging an elephant. Promptly they turned and charged us … When the Zulus turned on us I do not believe there was one man in the troop who was not in a mighty hurry to mount his horse – myself, of course, included' (Mossop 1937: 67).

From the camp, eyewitnesses had seen the Zulu skirmishers fall back under that first volley and the lines behind them press forward. The mounted men – Mossop among them – just managed to dash back to the main laager with the Zulu in pursuit, the first shells of the day passing over their heads to burst above the Zulu behind. The Zulu were shouting the war-cry, 'uSuthu!' and calling out in isiZulu 'We are the boys from iSandlwana!' Once the mounted men were clear, the infantry opened fire along the whole north side of the laager and redoubt:

An incident during the opening stage of the battle. As the sortie by British mounted troops provoked an attack by the Zulu right, Lt Edward Browne of the 24th Regiment (attached Mounted Infantry) won the Victoria Cross for saving the life of Lt Col J.C. Russell, who had failed to mount his horse in time. (Author's Collection)

It was a clear, calm, sunny day … The first lines of the Zulu wing we had led on to the attack struck the north line of wagons with a crash which could be heard above all the din, their shields held out in front and first hitting the line. True to their mode of surrounding the enemy, when the first lines struck the wagons those behind swung to the right and left, part charging along the east side of the wagons and part on the west … In a few minutes the whole west line was engaged, and it being a calm day, the smoke from the rifle fire began to bother us; we could barely distinguish the Zulus only a few feet away. Finding no opening, the Zulus turned and charged the whole line. Crash! – as their shields struck the wagons, and the whole line shook. 'They are in! They are in!' was shouted by the men under the wagons. Thrusting my head through my loop-hole [cut in the canvas of a wagon-tent] I could see dimly, through a haze of smoke, a heaving, struggling, black mass trying to wrench a couple of wagons from the line to make an opening, and others swarming over them … A company of the 13th Regiment, with fixed bayonets, turned up in support, other men came running up, and the Zulus were driven back … (Mossop 1937: 70)

In fact, it seems only the leading elements of the right 'horn' reached the laager since those further to their left came under a swathing fire that brought them to a halt. Perhaps hoping to employ their tactics of advancing in short rushes between throwing themselves down flat, the iNgobamakhosi had gone to ground. But there was little cover, and each attempt at a rush attracted a storm of fire. According to Mehlokazulu,

The English fired their cannon and rockets, and we were fighting and attacking them for about one hour. I mean the Ngobamakosi regiment. Before the main body of the Zulu army came up, we, when the Zulu army did come up, were lying prostrate – we were beaten, we could do no more. So many were killed that the few men who were not killed were lying between dead bodies, so thick were the dead. (Quoted in *NM Supp* 1879: 350)

Zofikasho Zungu, also of the iNgobamakhosi, agreed:

We were fired at from above by the soldiers in trenches. There were many 'bye and byes' [a Zulu term for artillery] and they fired pot-legs [meaning shrapnel] at us and we died in hundreds, and the paraffin [rockets] that was shot at us made a great noise and burnt [men] so badly they couldn't recognise who they were. I don't think we killed any soldiers as they were well entrenched … (Quoted in *SQ* Sep 1993: 16)

Those of the iNgobamakhosi and uVe who could find the slightest amount of cover on the exposed slope lay down and opened a heavy but inaccurate fire on the laager while the rest retired, taking advantage of the shelter of a rocky fold in the ground below the redoubt to regroup.

The noise of this first attack had brought the left 'horn', delayed by boggy ground along the stream-beds, hurrying up the valley south of the camp and up a steep grassy slope, which brought them out onto the ridge scarcely 100yd from the cattle-laager; only once they crested the rise onto the higher ground would they be exposed to British fire. As usual their advance was screened by their skirmishers. In particular, at the top of the slope off to the Zulu left, was a low mound covered with vegetation which was occupied by men of the uKhandempemvu. As Wood explained:

> Some 40 Zulus, using Martini-Henry rifles which they had taken at Isandwhlana [*sic*], occupied ground between the edge of the ravine and the rear of the Laager, from the fire of which they were partly covered by the refuse from the Horse Lines which had there been deposited, for, with the extraordinary fertility of South Africa, induced by copious rains and burning midday sun, a patch of mealies 4 feet high afforded cover to men lying down, and it was from thence that our serious losses occurred somewhat later. The Zulu fire induced me to withdraw a company of the 13th, posted at the right rear of the cattle Laager, although the front was held by another half company for some time longer. (Wood 1907: 381)

From this slightly elevated position the Zulu could fire directly across at the cattle-laager and, further off, at the redoubt. The distribution of the best part of 1,000 modern Martini-Henry rifles and carbines, captured at iSandlwana, certainly had a marked improvement on Zulu musketry at Khambula, and as one unidentified witness observed:

The Khambula battlefield today, looking from the site of the redoubt towards the main laager, which lay where the trees now stand. The Zulu right attacked up the slope from the right of this picture early in the battle; their repulse ensured that subsequent Zulu attacks would remain unco-ordinated, and allowed Wood to shift his artillery to each one in turn. (Author's Collection)

> … the volleys they delivered was something terrible, especially on the side where the 1/13th were stationed … Colour-Sergeant McAllen was wounded in the arm, and after the wound was dressed ran out to his company, performing his duty until shot dead. Acting Sergeant Quigley, R.A., exhibited great energy and zeal in working his gun in the fort, and did excellent service after his officer had been mortally wounded. Sergeant Brown, 80th Regiment, attached to Royal Artillery, exhibited similar energy and zeal in working the other gun in the fort, being severely wounded doing his duty. (Quoted in *NM Supp* 1879: 155)

A Sgt Jervis of the 90th Light Infantry commented that 'the bullets fell on the fort in which I was signalling in showers' (quoted in Emory 1977: 172). Under cover of this fire, men from the uNokhenke pushed up the slope and began to force a way into the cattle-laager, and skirmishing broke out among the press of cattle as the company of the 1/13th Light Infantry withdrew to the shelter of the main laager. It was a dangerous moment for the British, as Wood observed:

> A 13th man coming late from the cattle Laager, not having heard the order to retire, was shot by the Zulus lying in the refuse heap, and followed by four of them from the cattle Laager. I was running out to pick him up, when Captain Maude exclaimed, 'Really it isn't your place to pick up single men,' and went out himself, followed by Lieutenants Lysons and Smith, 90th Light Infantry; they were bringing the man in, who was shot in the leg, when, as they were raising the stretcher, Smith was shot through the arm … (Wood 1907: 381)

A Sgt Fisher of the 1/13th Light Infantry fell wounded and Pte Grosvenor stopped to help him away – but Grosvenor himself was too slow, and the Zulu already in the cattle-laager overtook him and killed him.

With the cattle-laager now in Zulu hands, the head of the slope leading up from the valley had been secured on both flanks and the uKhandempemvu and uMbonambi *amabutho* began to assemble lower down, out of reach from the British fire, for an assault. Wood saw the danger – that any such attack, being sheltered from fire until it emerged onto the higher ground, might not be exposed to rifle-fire for long enough for the British to disrupt it. Accordingly, he 'sent Captain Maude to order out two companies of the 90th, under Major Hackett, with instructions to double over the slope down to the ravine with fixed bayonets, and to fall back once they had driven the Zulus below the crest' (Wood 1907: 381). These companies would have to move across 200yd of open ground at the head of the slope and then deploy in the open, with the cattle-laager on their left and the dung-heaps further off on their right – both now occupied by the Zulu. In the event, Wood was impressed with their performance: '… the two companies 90th Light Infantry came out at a steady 'double' Major Hackett leading, guided by Captain Woodgate … Lieutenant Strong, who had recently joined us, ran well out in front of his company, sword in hand, and the Zulus retired into the ravine' (Wood 1907: 382).

One unidentified observer thought that Woodgate marched out 'as leisurely and unconcernedly as if he were pacing a piece of ground for cricket wickets' (quoted in *NM Supp* 1879: 155). Some of the leading Zulu at the top of the valley had to be driven back with the bayonet as the companies deployed in a skirmish line and opened a heavy fire on the Zulu below. The effect of this fire was undoubtedly discouraging, but Hackett's men were now swept with Zulu fire from both flanks in return: 'Major Hackett was shot through the head; [Lt] Arthur Bright fell mortally wounded and the Colour-Sergeant of Bright's company, [Mc]Allen, a clever young man, not 23 years of age, who had been

A Zulu man in the full ceremonial dress of his *ibutho*. Each *ibutho* had a distinct combination of feathers, furs and shield-colour, and this man is wearing a uniform and carrying a shield associated with the uKhandempemvu *ibutho*. These uniforms were worn at the great assembly of the army that accompanied the annual harvest ceremonies each year, but were too fragile and precious to be worn on prolonged campaigning. (Author's Collection)

Maj Robert Hackett, who led the sortie by two companies of the 90th Light Infantry to disrupt the Zulu left shortly after 1500hrs. (Royal Archives, Windsor Castle)

Khambula, 29 March 1879

British view: Worried by the ability of the Zulu left to mass sheltered from British fire in the valley south of the British camp, Col Wood has ordered two companies of the 90th Light Infantry under Maj Robert Hackett to leave the protection of the wagon-laager and move to a position at the head of the valley. Crossing ground already strewn with Zulu dead from earlier attacks, they have formed up in open order and have begun to fire on the Zulu no more than 100–200yd away.

On the left a squad is driving off at bayonet point Zulu who had lingered closer to the laagers. Yet Hackett's contingent is exposed to heavy Zulu flanking fire, however, both from Zulu who have successfully captured the cattle-laager (off to the left) and to those who have occupied the over-grown camp dung-heaps (right distance), and who have opened a well-directed fire with Martini-Henry rifles captured at iSandlwana.

Hackett himself falls to a shot which has passed clean through his head behind his eyes; of his subalterns, Lt Arthur Bright, would be mortally wounded and several others killed or wounded. Hackett's companies could not hold this position for long, and retreated to the main laager carrying their wounded with them.

Zulu view: The Zulu left 'horn' – the uKhandempemvu and uMbonambi *amabutho* – were regrouping away from the fire from the entrenched British positions when Hackett's men appeared at the head of the valley just above them, driving away those Zulu (right background) who had managed to shelter closer to the laagers. Packed closely together, preparing to charge, the Zulu are dangerously vulnerable to Hackett's close-range volleys.

An *induna*, an older man distinguished by his head-ring and crane-feather and carrying a status weapon, an axe, tries to urge the uMbonambi forward to attack, and the men crouch low in preparation, raising their shields against the British fire. Yet the short space ahead of them is too swept with British fire for them to cross; although Hackett will, in turn, be forced to retreat by supporting Zulu musketry, the incident badly disrupts the Zulu left and inflicts heavy casualties. The battle of Khambula will in the end demonstrate decisively that Zulu skill at close-range tactical assaults and hand-to-hand combat are no match for concentrated British firepower.

wounded in the first attack, and, having had his arm dressed, rejoined his company as it charged, was killed' (Wood 1907: 382).

The companies could not stay exposed to this fire for long. According to Capt Woodgate: 'At first the advance was successful, a large number of men giving way before the two companies and retiring from the crest down the slope. But coming under a heavy and well-directed cross-fire from other quarters, the two companies were ordered to retire, having lost two officers (Major Hackett and Lieutenant Bright) and about 25 men killed or wounded' (quoted in Emery 1977: 175). Hackett had been shot by a bullet that had entered one side of his head, behind the eyes, and passed clean through; his face was covered with blood and he appeared to be dead. His body was placed with others in the centre of the laager; later someone saw him move, and it was found that he was still alive. Remarkably the bullet had not seriously damaged his brain, but it had destroyed his optic nerves – he would recover from his terrible injuries, but would be blind for life.

Expecting the Zulu to follow up Hackett's retreat, Wood ordered the main laager to be prepared for another rush:

> A wagon was removed from near the south-west corner, and what they called a 'sortie' was made by an officer and a company [*sic*] of regulars to sweep a body of Zulus away with the bayonet. The Zulus promptly swept them back through the gap, and came in after them. A Zulu regiment had appeared like magic rushing up in support. Had the concentrated fire from the fort not kept them back they would have entered, and there would have been such a mess in the laager that the Zulus would have swept over the wagons in all directions … (Mossop 1937: 73)

The iconic image of the battle of Khambula – Hackett's sortie, sketched from eyewitness accounts by the war artist Melton Prior. Prior has shown the men carrying greatcoats – which is unlikely when defending a camp – but otherwise correctly shows them deployed in open order with the redoubt and laagers beyond. Note, too, the tents lying on the ground, left – struck when the Zulu first came into view. (Author's Collection)

Mbongoza, uMbonambi *ibutho*

Mbongoza fought with the uMbonambi throughout the conflict, including the battles of iSandlwana and Khambula. The men of the uMbonambi *ibutho* had been born about 1843, early in King Mpande's reign, and had spent their childhood as all Zulu boys did, looking after their father's livestock. They were hardy, self-reliant, and accustomed to accepting authority in a patriarchal society in which rights and privileges accrued with age. At some point about 1860 they had been called together to serve a few months of the year as cadets attached to their nearest royal homestead, and for the first time began to identify themselves as member of a fledgling group.

The men of the uMbonambi, like those of every *ibutho*, were bound together by a fierce sense of pride reflected in their own songs and war cries, and by a determination to excel in defence of their country and way of life. It was usual, in the ceremonies which preceded a campaign, for the king to set one *ibutho* to challenge another, individual warriors dancing out in public to boast of the heroic deeds they would perform in the coming fight, and to taunt their rivals: in the muster of January 1879 the uMbonambi challenged the uNokhenke, and the iNgobamakhosi the uKhandempemvu. It is no coincidence that all these *amabutho* would play a prominent part in the battles to come.

Mbongoza himself would survive the war and was still living to tell his story in 1929; by that time he was so completely identified with his old *ibutho* that he was known simply as Mbongoza uMbonambi.

Although Wood considered Hackett's sortie the decisive moment of the battle it had clearly been a close call. Yet the Zulu counter-attack faltered and the uKhandempemvu and uMbonambi again retired into the valley. Throughout the battle the four field guns working in the open had shifted their positions to

The wounded Maj Hackett is carried away as his companies retire to the protection of the main laager; Hackett was unconscious and his men placed him with the British dead until he was later seen to move. (Author's Collection)

Andrew Guthrie, 90th Light Infantry

Cpl Andrew Guthrie was typical of the ordinary British soldier of his day. Most, like him, had been driven to enlist by economic hardship, or as an escape from the hopelessness of their daily lives. At 5ft 8in tall Guthrie had been 2½in taller than the minimum height requirement, and most recruits, like him, were in their late teens or early twenties at the time of their enlistment. Although the Army generally preferred to recruit men from a rural background – whom it considered healthier and stronger – the huge social changes which had followed industrialization in the late 18th and early 19th centuries had led to a drift from the country to the towns, and by the 1870s the majority of recruits were recruited from urban areas. Moreover, the new short-service system had not yet completely transformed the nature of those recruits, and many battalions still had a high proportion of old long-service men working through. In the 1/24th, for example, the majority of men were in their late 20s – the prime of a soldier's life – in 1879, while those in the battalions sent out fresh from home as reinforcements, including Guthrie's 90th Light Infantry, were scarcely out of their teens. Nevertheless, at the start of the Zulu campaign, all but two battalions (the 2/4th and 99th, sent out at the very end of 1878) had been in southern Africa for some time and most, like Andrew Guthrie, had received combat experience.

meet each attack, and they now turned to fire upon the cattle-laager where members of the uNokhenke were still sheltering among the cattle, causing carnage among the Zulu and cattle alike. It was about now, too, that the British neutralized the danger posed by the dung-heaps, firing a series of volleys directly into the heap itself and hitting many of the Zulu sheltering behind; the following morning 62 bodies were found among the debris.

At 1730hrs Wood despatched Thurlow and Waddy's companies of the 13th Light Infantry 'to the right rear of the cattle Laager, to turn out some Zulus who were amongst the oxen, which they had, however, been unable to remove; and I took Captain Laye's company to the edge of the kranz on the

Men of Guthrie's unit, the 90th Light Infantry, in camp with Wood's No. 4 (Left Flank) Column. Note the effect of heavy campaigning on their uniforms – several have lost their helmets and replaced them instead with civilian hats. (Author's Collection)

A Zulu marksman – firing a British Martini-Henry captured at iSandlwana – snipes at the British mounted troops emerging to pursue the retreating Zulu at the end of the battle. The presence of captured modern weapons had greatly improved Zulu marksmanship throughout the clash at Khambula. (Author's Collection)

right front of the Laager, where they did great execution with the bayonet' (Wood 1907: 383). One unidentified eyewitness thought that 'G and F companies 1-13th charged them down the ravine at the point of the bayonet, hurling them headlong into holes, crevices, nooks, and corners of every description. At the same time the field-pieces were throwing case-shot, shrapnel, etc, into the midst of the retreating bodies of Zulus, causing great destruction of life' (quoted in *NM Supp* 1879: 160). From the camp the defenders could see many groups of two men helping away a wounded comrade between them.

At first the Zulu withdrawal was orderly, many warriors stopping as they walked to turn and fire. But Wood ordered out the mounted men who had suffered at Hlobane to drive away the retreating Zulu and inflict as many casualties as they could. The pursuit at Khambula displayed a degree of British ruthlessness in stark contrast to the aftermath of the earlier victory at Nyezane: 'When we overtook small bodies they made no attempt to resist; they were beaten, and that was the end. Many a man just turned, exposing his broad chest, saying "Dubula M'lungu" ("Shoot, white man") – and the white man shot' (Mossop 1937: 74).

Wood allowed the pursuit to continue until late evening before recalling his men, and there is no doubt it turned what had started as an orderly retreat into a rout. Once the shooting stopped the British took stock and looked to the plight of the wounded and dying. The battle of Khambula cost the British three officers and 26 men dead and five officers and 49 men wounded. By contrast, 785 Zulu bodies were collected from immediately around the laagers, loaded into wagons and carried to mass graves away from the camp, where they were hastily buried. Many of them showed signs of the terrible effectiveness of the concentrated British fire. Hundreds more bodies lay out on the line of retreat, and would never be buried, and even once the immediate confines of the camp had been cleared the grim residue remained:

A Zulu *inyanga* (herbalist doctor). Mgelija Ngema of the uVe, fighting at Khambula, still remembered his injuries more than 50 years later: 'I was shot here in my leg and my thigh and also here in the face … I sat and watched the fight until the soldiers came out and we ran away. I suffered great pain as my leg bone was shattered and many pieces of bone have come out, and it took me over a month to get back [home]' (quoted in *SQ* Sep 1993: 13). (Author's Collection)

> Now and then we get a sniff of the stench wafted towards the camp whenever the breeze blows from that direction. We had a heavy shower of rain yesterday, which was very acceptable, as it washed the brains and pools of blood that were saturating the ground down the hill and ravine, making the air smell a little sweeter. (Quoted in *NM Supp* 1879: 161)

Analysis & Conclusion

The battle of Khambula had marked a crucial break in British tactical thinking from the easy confidence with which they had begun the war. Lord Chelmsford – and the vast majority of the officers and men under his command – had entered the campaign convinced not only that their professional military discipline gave them an advantage over their supposedly unsophisticated Zulu enemies, but that British firepower was so overwhelmingly superior that the Zulu would be able to offer against it no credible defence. These impressions had largely been formed during the earlier British experience of the Eastern Cape Frontier campaign. Despite the fact that his intelligence had suggested from the very beginning that the Zulu fought differently, Chelmsford had remained convinced, as the invasion began, that he would have no difficulty in defeating them if only he could bring the Zulu to open battle.

'We are soldiers', runs the caption to this contemporary engraving; 'we have shown you how we can fight, and I'll show you how we can die'. The compassion displayed by British troops in victory had crumbled under the horrors of the defeat at iSandlwana, and later battles, including Khambula, were marked by a ruthless pursuit of the defeated enemy. (Author's Collection)

The open-order tactics that had succeeded on the Eastern Cape had indeed triumphed in Zululand under Pearson's direction at Nyezane, yet the disparity in casualties and apparent ease with which the Zulu were repulsed is misleading. Godide's army was tired after prolonged marching across the previous days, and was badly positioned for the attack as it in fact developed. Godide had enjoyed an uncharacteristically low numerical advantage for a Zulu commander, and his centre and right never became fully engaged, leaving Pearson to concentrate against the more enthusiastic attack of the Zulu left. Had the British had time to analyse the battle in more detail, they might have recognized that, while Pearson's command had been fully occupied dealing with just part of the Zulu force, it might have been acutely vulnerable to a more determined attack by the Zulu *amabutho* in their entirety.

In the event, however, the disaster at iSandlwana, occurring just a few hours after Nyezane, had emphasized these points with a greater and more terrible clarity. There, Ntshingwayo and Mavumengwana had enjoyed a greater numerical advantage, had seized the initiative at the beginning of the battle, and had dominated the terrain throughout. All of their *amabutho* had attacked with great determination, and the British line had in the end proved too extended to provide the impenetrable curtain of fire necessary to check them. Once the British line had collapsed, the Zulu strength at close-quarter combat had steadily broken up and destroyed all remaining resistance.

Nevertheless, still that same day, one final British success had pointed the way forward to their eventual triumph. At Rorke's Drift the small British garrison had been concentrated and shielded by barricades in such a way as to make it virtually impossible for the Zulu to exploit their tactical strengths – their excellent use of ground, their speed and manoeuvrability, their numbers and their sheer courage. At Rorke's Drift, kept at arm's length by nothing more than an improvised wall of mealie-sacks, the Zulu close-quarter fighting techniques had been rendered largely useless, to the extent that very few of the British casualties had been inflicted with spears. Although the Zulu had enjoyed a greater proportionate success with their musketry, this had been woefully ill-directed and served only to underline the Zulu over-dependence upon hand-to-hand weapons.

At Khambula the same tactical contest had been played out on a grander scale, and with far greater strategic consequences. Here the men of an entire British column were sheltered by barricades in much the same way as the garrison at Rorke's Drift, and proportionately even fewer casualties had fallen in hand-to-hand combat. Indeed, despite the extraordinary courage and tenacity of the Zulu attacks, the losses suffered by the British might have proved inconsequential had it not been for the improvement in Zulu firepower resulting from the deployment of British rifles captured earlier at iSandlwana. If the loose open lines that had worked so well for the British on the Eastern Cape Frontier had played to the Zulu strengths at iSandlwana, the tight British formations that had evolved by the middle of the war prompted a painful demonstration of their weaknesses. The Zulu had indeed, despite King Cetshwayo's warnings, 'put their faces into the lair of the wild beast' – and been clawed.

The battle would, as the king had feared, prove a decisive one, and it established the pattern for later British successes in the war. The elation of that first victory at iSandlwana gave way among the Zulu after Khambula to shock and a feeling of helplessness, and although the *amabutho* would dutifully assemble once again to depend the royal homesteads at oNdini, they would not fight in the same spirit again. To make matters worse, just a few days later at the battle of kwaGingindlovu, near the coast, local Zulu forces were just as unable to halt the advance of Lord Chelmsford's march to relieve Eshowe. Here, Chelmsford – taking direct command in battle for the first time during the campaign – had developed the growing British tactical advantage to its logical conclusion. He had formed his men in a square, four ranks deep on each side and protected by a shelter-trench and rampart. Although the square was a fighting technique which had largely been abandoned in conventional European warfare – where such concentrations were dangerously exposed to effective enemy return fire – it provided a curtain of fire on all sides which allowed the Zulu encircling tactics no purchase whatever. Furthermore, Chelmsford had reinforced the weakest parts of the square – the corners – with artillery, Gatling guns and rockets. Although the Zulu had attacked with such determination that some of their dead fell close to the shelter-trench, they did not manage to charge home. By June a heavily reinforced Chelmsford was ready to renew his advance on oNdini.

For the units who had played such a prominent part in the early battles of the war, the progress of the campaign brought mixed fortunes. After its success at Nyezane the 2/3rd Regiment had marched under Pearson to occupy Eshowe. Two companies were sent back to the Thukela escorting a convoy of empty wagons on 25 January, but the remaining six companies were invested with the rest of the column at Eshowe; the two detached companies later took part in the action of kwaGingindlovu. After Eshowe was relieved, the Buffs remained in the coastal sector, but saw no further action.

The uMxapho *ibutho*, which had attacked the Buffs so determinedly at Nyezane, very nearly succeeded in ambushing a detachment of Redvers Buller's mounted men on the plain close to oNdini on 3 July. The iNgobamakhosi and uKhandempemvu, who had fought so fiercely at both iSandlwana and Khambula, had also answered the call to assemble for the final battle, despite the losses they had already endured. It was the uKhandempemvu who, at the end of June, guarded the drifts across the White Mfolozi River – the last geographical obstacle to the British advance on oNdini – and who had refused to allow a herd of white cattle, sent by the king as a peace offering, to pass. They were not yet defeated, they said, and were not ready to accept such humiliation. The iNgobamakhosi, uMbonambi, uMxapho and uKhandempemvu all fought at the battle of Ulundi on 4 July.

So, too, did the 90th Regiment, which had defended the main wagon-laager against them at Khambula, and which remained part of Wood's column throughout the remainder of the war. The 1/24th Regiment, however, those experienced men who had been stationed for years at the Cape and who had served throughout the 1877–78 campaign before the invasion of Zululand, had been largely destroyed at iSandlwana. The battalion was reconstituted with recruits hurried out from a number of training depots in the UK, but there was scarcely time to build a new sense of belonging and identity before the war ended. Several times during the false alarms that marked the final advance on oNdini the 1/24th Regiment had proved unsteady, and Lord Chelmsford had refused to allow them to take part in the final battle; instead, they were left to guard his baggage train at a fort on the White Mfolozi.

When the British finally reached oNdini, and confronted Cetshwayo's *amabutho* for the last time at the battle they called Ulundi, Chelmsford again deployed in a square, this time fielding more troops than at any other battle in the war. So heavy was the British musketry, artillery, Gatling and rocket fire on all sides that it was not only hugely destructive to life but provided an assault on the senses of the attacking Zulu that was quite literally stunning. According to Sofikasho Zungu of the iNgobamakhosi,

> … there was one great roar of big guns. I could see flames of the guns and smoke from them, and also the flames of 'paraffin' [rockets] that I saw at Khambula. We soon broke and ran, there was such a roar of guns we were utterly bewildered. One shot went close to my head and I fell down and thought I was dead. I saw one [warrior] whose head was struck right off next to me and his body stood up shivering with arms clenched until it fell. (Quoted in *SQ* Sep 1993: 16)

Perhaps, in the final analysis, Lord Chelmsford had not been so wrong to place his faith in British firepower – but it had taken a number of harsh practical lessons before the British had best understood how to manage that asset. 'What could we do against you English?' asked one Zulu veteran after the war: 'You stand still, and only by turning something round [i.e. the handle of a Gatling gun] make bodies of our warriors fly to pieces; legs here, arms there, everything. Whouw! What can we do against that?' (quoted in Mitford 1883: 174).

The battle of Ulundi, on 4 July 1879. The lessons of Rorke's Drift and Khambula had led the British to abandon entirely the extended formations with which they had entered the war; instead, they reverted to the traditional Napoleonic square, which provided an impenetrable curtain of fire on all sides and effectively negated the Zulu encircling tactics. This is the closing stage of the battle; one face of the square has marched aside to allow the cavalry to emerge and complete the Zulu rout. (Author's Collection)

ORDERS OF BATTLE

Nyezane, 22 January 1879

First Division, No. 1 (Right Flank) Column (Col C.K. Pearson, 2/3rd Regiment)

Infantry: Five companies, 2nd Battalion, 3rd (East Kent) Regiment of Foot ('The Buffs') (Lt-Col H. Parnell; companies under Capt A.C. Jackson, Capt H.D. Harrison, Capt W.H. Wyld, Capt J.W. Forster and Lt R. Martin); seven companies, 1st Battalion, 2nd Regiment, Natal Native Contingent (Maj S. Graves, 3rd Regiment).

Mounted troops: No. 2 Squadron, Mounted Infantry (Maj P.H.S. Barrow, 19th Hussars); Natal Hussars (Capt P. Norton); Stanger Mounted Rifles (Capt F. Addison); Victoria Mounted Rifles (Capt C.T. Sauer).

Others: Detachment, Naval Brigade, HMS *Active* (Cdr H.J.F. Campbell RN; one .450in Gatling gun and two 24-pdr rocket tubes); detachment, No. 11 Battery, 7th Brigade, Royal Garrison Artillery (Lt W.N. Lloyd RA; two Mk IV 7-pdr RML field guns and one 9-pdr rocket trough); No. 2 Field Company, Royal Engineers (Capt W.R.C. Wynne RE); half-company, No. 2 Company, Natal Native Pioneers (Lt T.R. Main RE).

Second Division, No. 1 (Right Flank) Column (Lt-Col W.H.D.R. Welman, 99th Regiment)

Two companies, 2nd Battalion, 3rd (East Kent) Regiment of Foot ('The Buffs'); one company, 99th Duke of Edinburgh's (Lanarkshire) Regiment of Foot.

Zulu forces (Godide kaNdlela)

uMxapho *ibutho* (approx. 40 companies; *c.* 2,600 men); uDlambedlu and izinGulube *amabutho* (about 15 companies; *c.* 900 men); local elements from the iNsukamgeni, iQwa, uDududu and iNdabakawombe *amabutho* (about 50 companies; *c.* 2,500 men).

iSandlwana, 22 January 1879

Detachment, No. 2 Column (Bvt Col A.W. Durnford)

Infantry: D Company, 1st Regiment, Natal Native Contingent (Capt C. Nourse); E Company, 1st Regiment, Natal Native Contingent (Capt W. Stafford).

Mounted troops (Capt W. Barton): No. 1 Troop, Sikhali (amaNgwane) Horse (Lt C. Raw); No. 2 Troop, Sikhali (amaNgwane) Horse (Lt J. Roberts); No. 3 Troop, Sikhali (amaNgwane) Horse (Lt R. Vause); Hlubi (Tlokoa) Troop (Lt A. Henderson); Edendale Troop (Lt H.D. Davies).

Others: Detachment, No. 11 Battery, 7th Brigade, Royal Artillery (Bvt Maj F.B. Russell; three 9-pdr rocket troughs).

Detachment, No. 3 (Centre) Column (Lt-Col Henry B. Pulleine)

Infantry: Five companies, 1st Battalion, 24th (2nd Warwickshire) Regiment of Foot (Capt W. Degacher; comprised A Company under Lt F. Porteous; C Company under Capt R. Younghusband; E Company under Lt C.W. Cavaye; F Company under Capt W. Mostyn; H Company under Capt G. Wardell); G Company, 2nd Battalion, 24th (2nd Warwickshire) Regiment of Foot (Lt C. Pope; included a number of unattached men); two companies, 1st Battalion, 3rd Regiment, Natal Native Contingent (comprised No. 6 Company under Capt R. Krohn and No. 9 Company under Capt J. Lonsdale); two companies, 2nd Battalion, 3rd Regiment, Natal Native Contingent (comprised No. 4 Company under Capt E. Erskine and No. 5 Company under Capt A. Barry).

Mounted troops: Detachment, No. 1 Squadron, Mounted Infantry; detachment, Natal Mounted Police; detachment, Natal Carbineers (Lt F. Scott); detachment, Newcastle Mounted Rifles (Capt R. Bradstreet); detachment, Buffalo Border Guard (QM D. Macphail).

Others: Detachment, N Battery, 5th Brigade, Royal Artillery (Bvt Maj St. Smith; two Mk IV 7-pdr RML field guns); detachment, Army Service Corps; detachment, Army Hospital Corps; detachment, No. 1 Company, Natal Native Pioneer Corps; detachment, 90th Regiment of Foot (Perthshire Volunteers) (Light Infantry).

Zulu forces (Ntshingwayo kaMahole and Mavumengwana kaNdlela)

Right 'horn': uDududu, iMbube and iSangqu *amabutho*.

'Chest': uNokhenke, uKhandempemvu (uMcijo) and uMbonambi *amabutho*.

Left 'horn': iNgobamakhosi and uVe *amabutho*.

Reserve (Zibhebhu kaMapitha (WIA); Prince Dabulamanzi kaMpande): uThulwana, iNdlondlo, uDloko and iNdluyengwe *amabutho*.

Some companies of the uMxapho (who were otherwise fighting at Nyezane the same day) had joined the army on its march, as had numbers of men from various other *amabutho* who had not attended the initial muster but had rallied to the *impi* as it passed through the country.

Khambula, 29 March 1879

No. 4 (Left Flank) Column (Bvt Col H. E. Wood vc)

Infantry: seven companies, 1st Battalion, 13th (1st Somersetshire) (Prince Albert's Light Infantry) Regiment of Foot (Lt-Col P. Gilbert); eight companies, 90th Regiment of Foot (Perthshire Volunteers) (Light Infantry) (Bvt Lt-Col R. Rogers).

Mounted troops (Lt-Col R. Buller): No. 1 Squadron, Mounted Infantry (Lt-Col J.C. Russell); four troops, Frontier Light Horse (Capt C. D'Arcy); two troops, Raaf's Transvaal Rangers (Cdt Pieter Raaf); Baker's Horse (Cdt J.F. Baker); Kaffrarian Rifles (Cdt F. Schermbrucker); Edendale Troop (Lt W. Cochrane).

Others: No. 11 Battery, 7th Brigade, Royal Artillery (Maj E.G. Tremlett; six 7-pdr guns and two rocket troughs); auxiliaries (Wood's Irregulars) (Maj W. Leet); detachment, Royal Engineers.

Zulu forces (overall commander Mnyamana kaNqengelele; field commander Ntshingwayo kaMahole)

Right 'horn': iNgobamakhosi and uVe *amabutho.*

'Chest': uDududu, iSangqu, iMbube, uThulwana, iNdlondlo, uDloko and iNdluyengwe *amabutho.*

Left 'horn': uKhandempemvu, uMbonambi and uNokhenke *amabutho.*

These *amabutho* were supported by a strong contingent from the abaQulusi, the people who lived around Hlobane Mountain, and who were not incorporated into the *amabutho* system but fought as a separate unit of their own.

BIBLIOGRAPHY

Castle, Ian (2003). *British Infantryman in South Africa 1877–81.* Oxford: Osprey Publishing.

Castle, Ian & Knight, Ian (1994). *Fearful Hard Times: The Siege and Relief of Eshowe 1879.* London: Greenhill Books.

Colenso, Frances & Durnford, Edward (1880). *History of the Zulu War and its Origins.* London: Chapman & Hall.

Emery, Frank (1977). *The Red Soldier: Letters from the Zulu War, 1879.* London: Hodder & Stoughton.

Hamilton-Browne, G. (1912). *A Lost Legionary in South Africa.* London: Werner Laurie.

Hart-Synnot, Maj Gen Fitzroy, ed. B.M. Hart-Synnot (1912). *Letters of Major-General Fitzroy Hart-Synnot.* London: E. Arnold.

Knight, Ian (1990). *Brave Men's Blood: The Epic of the Zulu War, 1879.* London: Greenhill Books.

Knight, Ian (1991). *British Forces in Zululand 1879.* London: Osprey Publishing.

Knight, Ian (1995a). *The Anatomy of the Zulu Army, from Shaka to Cetshwayo.* London: Greenhill Books.

Knight, Ian (1995b). *Zulu 1816–1906.* Oxford: Osprey Publishing.

Knight, Ian (1996). *Go To Your God Like A Soldier: The British Soldier Fighting for Empire.* London: Greenhill Books.

Knight, Ian (2010). *Zulu Rising: The Epic Story of iSandlwana and Rorke's Drift.* London: Macmillan.

Laband, John (1995). *Rope of Sand: The Rise and Fall of the Zulu Kingdom in the Nineteenth Century.* Johannesburg: Jonathan Ball.

Macdougall, Andrew Guthrie (1998). *The Guthrie Saga, Including the Diary of Andrew J. Guthrie 1877–1883.* Bishop Auckland: Pentland Press.

Mitford, Bertram (1883). *Through The Zulu Country: Its Battlefields And Its People.* London: Kegan Paul, Trench & Co.

Molyneux, Maj Gen W.C.F. (1896). *Campaigning in South Africa and Egypt.* London: Macmillan.

Moodie, D.C.F. (1888). *The History of the Battles and Adventures of the British, The Boers and the Zulus etc in Southern Africa.* 2 vols. Cape Town: Murray & St Leger.

Mossop, George (1937). *Running the Gauntlet: Some Recollections of Adventure.* London: T. Nelson & Sons.

Smith-Dorrien, Sir H.L. (1925). *Memories of Forty-Eight Years' Service.* London: J. Murray.

Stafford, Walter (1939). Unpublished typescript account, Talana Museum, KwaZulu-Natal.

Symons, J.P. (no date). 'My Reminiscences of the Zulu War'. Unpublished typescript, Campbell Collections, University of Natal.

Wood, Sir H. Evelyn (1907). *From Midshipman to Field Marshal.* London: Methuen.

Webb, C. de B. & Wright, J.B. (1976–2001). *The James Stuart Archive of Recorded Oral Evidence Relating to the History of the Zulu and Neighbouring Peoples.* 5 vols. Pietermaritzburg & Durban: University of Natal Press.

Wynne, W.R.C., ed. H. Whitehouse (1995). *A Widow-Making War: The Life and Death of a British Officer in Zululand, 1879.* Nuneaton: Paddy Griffith Associates.

Plus various newspapers and periodicals including: *Ilanga Lase Natal* (*Ilanga*); *Natal* magazine (*Natal*); *Natalia*; *Natal Mercury* (*NM*); *Natal Mercury Zulu War Supplement* (*NM Supp*); *Natal Witness* (*NW*); *Soldiers of the Queen, The Journal of the Victorian Military Society* (*SQ*).

INDEX

References to illustrations are shown in **bold**.